Newfoundland Christmas Cook Book

Published by:
HILLCREST PUBLISHING
St. John's, Newfoundland and Labrador

P.O. Box 5492, St. John's, NL A1C 5W4
2nd printing - 1984
3rd printing - 1985
4th printing - 1988 (revised)
5th printing - 1989
6th printing - 1992
7th printing - 1996
8th printing - 2002
9th printing - 2006
10th printing - 2010

Cover Design by Gary Manning

Table of Contents

Main Dishes

Roasting Turkey

TURKEY TIPS

When buying a turkey, allow approx. 1 lb. per person (this allows for seconds).

Defrosting: Defrost in one of the following ways:

1. Refrigerator Method: Leave turkey in original plastic bag on large tray. Pierce bag and allow abou 5 hours per pound.
2. Cold Water Method: Leave turkey in original plastic bag. Place in sink or large container. Cover with cold water, changing periodically. Allow about one hour per pound for thawing.
3. Room Temperature: Leave turkey in plastic covering. Place in a large brown paper bag. Close securely and allow about 1-1½ hours per pound.

To Prepare Turkey For Roasting: Remove gizzard, heart and liver from cavity (keep for gravy). Rinse inside and out with cold running water. Pat dry. Season cavity with salt and pepper. Because of the danger of food poisoning, DO NOT STUFF THE BIRD UNTIL JUST PRIOR TO ROASTING, or cook dressing in a separate container. Allow about one cup of stuffing for every 2 lbs. of turkey. Fill cavity loosely, allowing for expansion. If cooking dressing separately, place in a greased casserole, cover and put it in oven during the last 40 minutes of roasting. For a moist stuffing add some of the turkey drippings.

You can also cook the turkey on Christmas Eve, just roast up to within one hour of completion, then remove from oven and immediately remove stuffing and refrigerate. Store turkey covered with wet towels in refrigerator. The next day return both the dressing and turkey to oven and complete roasting time.

To Roast: Place bird, breast side up, on rack in roaster. Tie legs together and secure wings under back. Brush entire surface with melted margarine. Cover with a loose tent of foil – dull side out. Remove during the last hour. Baste periodically. Because turkeys vary due to conformation, variety, etc., cooking times are only approximate. Therefore it is very important to check for doneness often during the last hour of roasting. The most accurate test is with a meat thermometer. Insert into centre of inside thigh muscle, making sure thermometer does not touch the bone. It should register 180°-185°F. You may also check for doneness by inserting the point of a small paring knife into the thickest part of the thigh. The juices feel soft when pressed between fingers protected by paper towels. The leg should twist easily in its socket. When bird is cooked, place on platter, covered with foil to keep warm. Remove stuffing immediately. Let turkey stand for 20-30 minutes before carving.

TIMETABLE FOR ROASTING TURKEY AT 325°F

Ready to Cook Weight	Approximate Cooking Time	Approximate Amt. of Stuffing
6 - 8 lbs.	2½-3½ hours	3-4 cups
8 - 12 lbs.	3½-4½ hours	4-6 cups
16 - 20 lbs.	4½-5½ hours	8-10 cups
20 - 24 lbs.	5-6½ hours	10-12 cups

Whole, unstuffed turkey: allow about ½ hour less.
Meat thermometer reading: 180°-185°F

METRIC CONVERSIONS

1 tsp. — 5 ml	1 cup — 250 ml
½ tsp. — 2 ml	½ cup — 125 ml
¼ tsp. — 1 ml	¼ cup — 50 ml
1 tbsp. — 15 ml	1 lb. — 500 g
2 cups — 500 ml	2.2 lbs. — 1 kg
1½ cups — 375 ml	

OVEN TEMPERATURES*

300°F — 150°C	400°F — 200°C
325°F — 160°C	425°F — 220°C
350°F — 180°C	450°F — 230°C
375°F — 190°C	

*Always pre-heat your oven before baking. Oven temperatures vary due to age, etc., therefore it is wise to check your oven temperature from time to time using a reliable oven thermometer.

Basic Bread Dressing

Allow approx. 1 cup of dressing per 2 lb. of fowl. Day old bread is best.

6-8 cups of bread crumbs
1 lg. chopped onion
salt & pepper to taste
½ cup butter or margarine
4 tsp. Newfoundland savory

Combine crumbs, onion, seasonings, savory in a large bowl. Rub in butter with hands until well blended. Pack lightly into fowl. Sew filled cavity by stitching both ends of edges together with a darning needle and heavy thread, or close with poultry skewers and lace with string.

NOTE: May also be cooked separately in a covered casserole, during last 35-45 minutes adding some pan juices from time to time, or microwave on HI (covered) for 5-10 minutes, stirring occasionally.

Great-Grandmother's Turkey Stuffing

1 lb. bulk pork sausage
8 cups day-old bread cubes (16 slices)
1½ tsp. savory
¼ tsp. pepper
3 medium-size onions, chopped (1½ cups)
1 tbsp. dried parsley flakes
1 tsp. salt
1 can (about 17 oz.) cream-style corn

Cook sausage in a large skillet, stirring to break up, until browned. Remove from skillet. Pour off all but ¼ cup sausage fat. (Add vegetable oil if necessary to make ¼ cup.) Cook onions in fat until soft.

Combine bread cubes with parsley, savory, salt and pepper in a large bowl. Add onion mixture, sausage and corn and toss until well blended.

Note: If you have any stuffing left after stuffing the turkey, refrigerate. Form into 2-inch balls. Bake in pan around turkey the last 30 minutes of roasting. Place in shallow pan and keep warm in oven until dinner is ready.

Makes 10 cups.

Turkey Giblet Gravy

Giblets and neck from turkey
1 tsp. salt
½ cup chopped celery
½ cup flour
4¾ cups water
1 onion, slice fine
½ cup drippings from roasting pan

Wash giblets and neck, place all but liver in saucepan; add water, salt, onion and celery. Cover and bring to boil, then simmer until gizzard is tender — about three hours, adding liver five minutes ahead of this. Remove giblets and neck, strain broth — there should be four cups. Chop giblets and neck meat, discarding the gristly bits of gizzard. Blend drippings and flour together, stir in broth until thick, add giblets and heat through, stirring. Serve piping hot.

Homestyle Cranberry Sauce

1 pk. fresh or frozen cranberries
1 cup dry red wine
1 cup sugar
2 teaspoons cornstarch

Combine cranberries, sugar and ¾ cup of the wine in a medium size saucepan. Cook over medium heat, stirring occasionally, until cranberries just start to pop their skins.

Dissolve cornstarch in remaining ¼ cup wine. Stir into cranberry mixture, just until sauce thickens and bubbles. Cool. Chill.

Serve with turkey or cold meats.

Crystal Mint Jelly

1 cup creme de menthe liqueur
¼ cup fresh strained lime juice
¾ cup water
2½ cups sugar
½ bottle liquid pectin

Place first four ingredients into a large heavy saucepan. Bring to a boil over medium heat, stirring often, until sugar is completely dissolved. Let boil vigorously, stirring continuously for about one minute. Remove from heat and immediately stir in pectin. Skim off foam. Quickly pour into hot, sterilized jars and seal tightly. When cool, refrigerate.

Very nice accompaniment for your Christmas dinner.

Turkey Soup

Break apart carcass from leftover turkey and place in a large pot with any remaining meat. Cover with about 6-8 cups of water. Simmer over medium heat until meat falls from bones. Remove bones. Cut up large pieces of turkey into cubes. Return to pot. Add the following vegetables:

1 large chopped onion
1 cup diced celery
1 large carrot (chopped)
1 medium turnip (chopped)
⅓ cup barley or rice
⅓ cup soup noodles (optional)
salt and pepper to taste

Continue cooking over medium heat until vegetables are tender, about 1 hour or more. Serve and enjoy.

Turkey Noodle Casserole

¼ cup butter
1½ tsp. salt
2 cups light cream
2 tbsp. butter
⅓ cup chopped green pepper
2 tbsp. chopped onion
3 cups cooked noodles
¼ cup flour
1 cup turkey broth
3-4 tbsp. sherry (optional)
1 cup sliced mushrooms (canned pieces)
2½ cups diced cooked turkey
½ cup slivered toasted almonds

Heat oven to 350°F. Melt ¼ cup butter — blend in flour and salt and let bubble up together. Remove from heat. Add broth and cream. Stir to blend. Return to moderate heat and cook, stirring constantly, until thick and smooth. Heat 2 tbsp. butter and cook mushrooms, green pepper and onion in it until tender. Add to sauce along with noodles (and sherry). Pour into greased casserole or 13x9½" baking pan. Sprinkle with almonds. Bake 30 minutes.

Serves 8.

Turkey Salad

4 cups diced cooked turkey
1 cup sliced celery
⅓ cup chopped green onion
1 cup mayonnaise
2 cups diced sweet mixed pickles
½ pint cherry tomatoes, halved
½ cup slivered almonds, toasted
1½ tsp. salt

Combine all ingredients. Toss lightly to mix. Serve on lettuce.

Makes 6-8 servings.

Turkey Pot Pie

1 Recipe for 9" double pie crust
1 cup cooked cubed potato
1 onion, thinly sliced
2½ tbsp. flour
1 tbsp. crushed chicken bouillon cubes
1 tsp. parsley flakes
salt and pepper to taste
1 cup milk
⅓ cup water
1½ cups cooked cubed turkey
½ cup frozen green peas
½ cup frozen carrots
1 tin mushrooms, drained & sliced

Saute onion in about 3 tbsp. corn oil until tender. Stir in flour, bouillon granules, parsley flakes, salt and pepper. Blend in milk and water. Cook over moderate heat, stirring constantly, until thickened and bubbly. Remove from heat. Add turkey and vegetables. Set aside. Prepare pastry and fit into a 9" pie plate. Fill with the turkey mixture. Top with remaining pastry. Flute edges. Cut slits in top. Brush with egg white. Pre-heat oven to 425°. When ready place pie in oven and immediately turn down heat to 325°F and continue to bake for 40-60 minutes or until filling is hot and crust flaky.

Serve with a tossed salad.

Turkey Burgers

2 cups minced turkey
3 tbsp. bread crumbs
2 tbsp. water
1 egg
salt and pepper to taste
pinch of savory

Combine turkey and bread crumbs in a large bowl. Beat egg and water together, add to turkey mixture. Add seasonings and mix together well.

Shape into patties. Broil 3-4 minutes on each side.

Place on toasted buns. Serve with lettuce and tomato for a nutritious snack.

— TIP —

To prevent onion odor on your hands while slicing onions, rub a little vinegar on your fingers before and after slicing. The vinegar washed off easily.

Cranberry Relish Mold

1 pk. (3 oz.) raspberry-flavored gelatin
1 pk. (3 oz.) lemon-flavored gelatin
½ cup sugar
2 cups boiling cranberry juice cocktail
1 cup cold water
1 can (8 oz.) crushed pineapple
1 tbsp. lemon juice
2 cups fresh or frozen cranberries
1 unpeeled small orange, quartered and seeded
1 cup chopped celery
½ cup chopped walnuts

Combine raspberry and lemon gelatins with sugar in a large bowl. Pour boiling cranberry juice cocktail over, stirring to dissolve. Stir in cold water, undrained pineapple and lemon juice. Chill until as thick as unbeaten egg white.

Put cranberries and orange through food grinder. Combine with celery and nuts. Fold into gelatin mixture. Pour into an 8½-cup mold or a 12x7½x2-inch baking dish. Chill until firm. Unmold onto serving platter. Garnish with celery tops and sugared whole cranberries, if you wish.

Note: To make sugared cranberries, beat 1 egg white slightly; dip cranberries in egg white and roll in sugar. Let dry on paper toweling.

May be served with your Christmas dinner.

Makes 10 servings.

Port Wine Jelly

1 cup strained grapefruit juice (strain fresh)
1 bottle Certo
1 cup port wine
3½ cups sugar

Stir together juice, wine, and sugar. Place on low heat and stir until all sugar is dissolved. Mixture should be almost to a boil. Remove from heat, stir in the Certo, pour into glasses and let set.

Note: May be used with any meat dish. Could replace traditional Cranberry Sauce.

— TIP —

Fruit flavoured wine-vinegar — add preserves or jams to a jar of whole wine vinegar and let stand for a few days. Use in salad dressing or add a little cream to it to make a sauce for meat and chicken.

Festive Glazed Baked Ham

Scrub skin well with cold water. Place ham fat side up in a pan. Bake at 300°F (approx. 25-30 min. per lb.) according to type or directions if ham is partly cooked.

Remove from oven. Remove rind. Score the fat in diamonds — do not cut too deeply.

Stick **a whole clove** in the center of each diamond.

Glaze with the following.

Brush fat with ½ **cup corn syrup or honey.** Combine: **1 cup lightly packed brown sugar, 2 tbsp. flour, 1 tbsp. dry mustard.** Add vinegar to make a thick paste.

Spread over surface of ham. Fasten pineapple slices and maraschino cherries to ham with toothpicks.

Place in preheated 500°F oven for 10-15 min. to brown glaze. Baste frequently with syrup mixture that drips into pan.

Remove from oven and continue to baste for 10 min.

Glaze should be firm enough now to hold pineapple and cherries without toothpicks.

Glazes for Baked Ham

Orange-Honey: Combine ½ cup honey, ½ cup orange juice, and 1 cup light brown sugar; mix well.

Currant Jelly: Blend together 1 cup currant jelly, ½ tsp. dry mustard, and 2 tsp. prepared horseradish.

Cranberry: Fork whip 1 cup canned cranberry jelly with ½ cup light corn syrup.

Mustard: Combine 1 cup light brown sugar, ¼ cup prepared yellow mustard, and ½ tsp. powered cloves.

Split Pea Soup

2 cups split peas (dried)
12 cups cold water
1 lg. ham bone
1 lg. onion (chopped)
1 cup diced celery
1 cup diced turnip
½ cup diced parsnip
1 cup diced carrots
3 tbsp. butter
3 tbsp. flour

Let peas soak in cold water overnight. Next day place in a large pot and add the remaining ingredients. Cover and simmer for 2½-3 hours or until peas are tender. Remove ham bone and cut off meat. Return to pot add 3 tbsp. of butter and flour to 1 cup of the soup. Blend well and slowly pour into the soup pot. Simmer stirring until thickened.

Serve with fresh hot buttered rolls.

Ham and Scalloped Potatoes

3-4 tbsp. margarine
2 tbsp. chopped onion
2 tbsp. chopped green pepper
1 tbsp. chopped celery

In a heavy skillet melt the margarine. Saute vegetables until tender. Set aside while preparing the following sauce:

2 tbsp. cornstarch
2 cups milk
1 tsp. worchestershire sauce
½ tsp. salt
dash pepper
1 tsp. mustard
few drops tabasco sauce
2 cups sliced red potatoes
2 cups cubed ham
buttered bread crumbs
grated cheese

In a heavy saucepan, combine cornstarch with a little milk. Gradually add remaining milk. Cook over moderate heat, stirring occasionally until sauce begins to thicken. Add remaining ingredients. Combine well. Blend in the sauteed vegetables.

Butter a 1½-2 qt. casserole. Peel and slice 2 cups raw red potatoes.

Beginning with potatoes, alternate layers of potatoes, ham and sauce mixture. Top with buttered crumbs and cheese.

Bake uncovered in a 375°F oven for one hour. Uncover and bake another 15 minutes.

Christmas Goose

When buying a goose for roasting, allow about 1 pound "ready-to-cook" weight per serving. Goose varies in "ready-to-cook" weight from 4 to 14 pounds. If frozen, allow time for thawing.

To prepared and stuff the goose, follow directions given for turkey.

Use Nut and Fruit Stuffing below or your own favorite recipe. Insert a meat thermometer so tip rests in center of stuffing. Roast in a moderately low oven, 325°F. Place bird, breast side down, on a rack in a shallow pan or open roaster. Roast uncovered. Prick skin with a fork, sprinkle with salt. Pour off excess fat as it accumulates. Cook until well done - 185°F on a meat thermometer.

For a bird 4 to 8 lbs., allow 2¾ to 3½ hours; 8 to 12 lbs., 3½ to 4½ hrs.; 12 to 14 lb., about 4¾ hrs.

Nut and Fruit Stuffing

2 cups bread stuffing
3 ripe bananas, mashed
2 oranges, sectioned
1 cup broken walnut meats
2 tart apples, pared, cored and diced
1 cup halves, seeded grapes

Prepare bread stuffing. Blend in bananas. Add remaining ingredients; mix well. Makes about 3½ quarts, enough for a 14-pound goose.

Boxing Day Scallop Casserole

2-12 oz. pks. frozen scallops
2 tbsp. butter
½ cup milk
½-1 tsp. curry powder
1 cup shredded sharp processed Canadian cheese
2 tbsp. butter or margarine, melted
¼ cup chopped onion
1-10½ oz. can cream mushroom soup
dash pepper
1 can green beans
1 cup soft bread crumbs

Simmer scallops in boiling salted water 3-4 mins., drain, cook onion in 2 tbsp. butter 'til tender - not brown. Add soup, milk, curry powder, pepper and ½ cup of the cheese. Stir until cheese melts. Slice cooked scallops cross-wise. Combine with drained green beans in 10x6x1½ inch baking dish.

Pour soup mixture over. Sprinkle with remaining cheese, bread crumbs and 2 tbsp. butter. Bake in hot oven 425°F for 15-20 minutes.

Dave's Crab Quiche

1 9-inch baked pie shell
1 cup grated swiss cheese
1 cup fresh crab or 1 can (drained & flaked)
¼ cup chopped green onion
2 large eggs (beaten)
½ cup light cream
½ cup milk
¼ tsp. grated lemon
¼ tsp. dry mustard
dash nutmeg
¼ tsp. salt
¼ cup halved almonds

Place cheese over bottom of pie shell. Add crab and onion. Whisk eggs, add cream, milk, grated lemon rind, and seasonings. Pour over crab and top with almonds.

Bake in a pre-heated, 325°F oven for 45 minutes.

— TIP —

Going to a pot luck supper? Here's a tip: Wrap and tape casseroles in thick layers of newspapers. Will keep hot for about four hours.

Christmas Eve Fish Chowder

1 lb. cod or sole
⅓ cup onions
1 cup carrots
3 cups water
⅛ tsp. pepper
pinch sugar
2 tbsp. butter
2 cups diced potato
1 cup celery
2 tsp. salt
6 oz. tin condensed evaporated. milk

Place first 10 ingredients in pot (omit cod). Boil gently until cooked. Add fish. Simmer 10 mins. or until fish is cooked. Add milk. Re-heat, but **do not** boil. Shrimp, mussels, crab, may also be added if preferred.

P.S. Nice change from turkey and ham!

Holiday Cod Au Gratin

4 tbsp. butter
2 tbsp. flour
1 tsp. salt
½ tsp. pepper
2 cups milk
2½ cups fresh cod fish, cooked flaked, cooled
1 cup grated cheese

Melt butter. Add flour, salt and pepper. Stir to make a paste. Add milk and cook until it thickens, stirring constantly. Grease a 2 quart casserole. Pour a little of the sauce over the bottom. Add a layer of cod fish. Sprinkle with cheese. Repeat these layers until all ingredients are used, ending with a layer of cheese. Bake at 350°F until nicely browned, about 20 minutes.

Individual dishes may be used.

— TIP —

Sandwiches can be prepared beforehand and frozen. Avoid those fillings using hard cooked egg whites or raw vegetables. Egg whites develop a rubbery texture and vegetables lose their crispness.

Flippers for the Festive Season

2 frozen flippers
1 tbsp. baking soda
1 tsp. vinegar
½ doz. thick pieces fat-back pork
Pastry (see recipe below)
¼ cup butter
salt and pepper to taste
2 med. sized sliced onions
2 cups diced carrots and turnip

Clean flippers thorougly. Soak 1 hr. in boiling water containing soda and vinegar. Drain. Rinse flippers thoroughly, changing water 3 or 4 times.

Fry out pork and add butter. Brown flippers on both sides in fat. Add salt and pepper and sliced onions. Remove from frying pan and place in roaster. Cover flippers with water and cook at 400°F until boiling. Reduce heat to 350°F and continue baking 1½ hours.

Add vegetables and cook 3/4 hour longer.

Cover with pastry and bake until golden brown. Remove from roaster and thicken gravy. (A welcome change from turkey.)

PASTRY:
4 cups flour
½ lb. butter
1 cup water
4 tsp. baking powder
1 tsp. salt

Mix dry ingredients together. Cut in butter. Add water gradually. Stir with fork. Shape into soft ball and roll to desired shape.

After Christmas Meat Pie

Delicious hot, served with your favourite coleslaw, french fries and greens. Also good cold, served with your favourite salad or rice.

Make a pie crust pastry.

1 lb. ground beef or hamburger
1 med. onion (diced)
a little savory (if desired)
1 or 2 Oxo cubes (dissolve in boiling water)
salt and pepper (to taste)

Cook meat slowly, stir well. Add onion, salt, pepper and savory. Thicken this mixture with 3 or 4 tsp. flour. Pour into prepared pie dish, top with pastry. Cook 20-25 minutes or until slightly brown.

Roast Beef and Yorkshire Pudding

1 8-10 lb. rib roast (bone in)

Insert a meet thermometer into thickest part of meat. Place fat side up in roasting pan and place in a 450°F oven for 15-20 minutes.

Reduce heat to 325°F and continue cooking until meat thermometer registers desired doneness (see table below). Season half way through cooking time. Remove and let stand for 15 minutes (cover with foil) before carving.

Meanwhile prepare the Yorkshire Pudding as follows:

1 cup flour
½ tsp. salt
2 eggs (beaten)
1 cup milk
2 tbsp. fat drippings from roast

Combine flour and salt. Beat eggs until thick, stir in milk. Make a well in centre of flour mixture and pour in egg mixture. Beat at low speed until smooth. Chill. (May be prepared ahead of time while roast is cooking.)

Spoon some hot fat drippings into individual muffin pans or in a 9x13 inch pan. Heat until fat sizzles. Pour in batter and bake at 450°F for 15-20 minutes or until puffed and golden brown. Reduce heat to 350°F and cook about 15 minutes more. Serve immediately with roast beef.

Roasting Table

Well Done: 20 minutes per pound, or 160°F-170°F on meat thermometer.
Medium: 15 minutes per pound, or 150°F-160°F on meat thermometer.
Rare: 12 minutes per pound, or 130°F-140°F on meat thermometer.

Festive Meat Roll

1½ lbs. ground beef
½ cup tomato juice
2 eggs, beaten
½ cup soft bread crumbs
1½ tsp. salt
½ tsp. freshly ground black pepper
¼ tsp. oregano
2 cloves garlic, minced
3 tbsp. minced parsley
8 slices cooked ham
8 slices mozzarella cheese

Mix together all the ingredients but the ham and cheese. Cut a piece of waxed paper sixteen inches long. Pat out the meat mixture on it into a 10x16 inch rectangle. Arrange the ham and cheese on the meat, then roll up like a jelly roll, using the paper to help. Place in a greased loaf pan. Bake in a 350°F oven 1 hour.

Truly delicious!

Serves 6-8.

Holiday Mincemeat Pie

(A must for the Festive Season)

You may make your own mincemeat from scratch or use a commercially prepared type.

1 recipe for a 9" double crust pie

Mincemeat: (meatless)

12 apples, peeled and finely chopped
3 cups currants
1 tsp. ground nutmeg
1 tsp. cinnamon
¼ cup melted margarine
2 lemons
4 cups brown sugar
4 cups raisins
½ tsp. ground cloves
1 tsp. salt
2-4 tbsp. brandy (optional)

Grate lemon peels and squeeze juice in large bowl. Add peel. Chop the apples and toss lightly with lemon mixture (this prevents browning).

Add the remaining ingredients. Mix well. Put in sterilized jars and keep in a cool place. Use in your favorite tart recipe.

Place filling in a 9 inch pastry lined pie plate. Place pastry over top. Slit top. Bake 400°F for 25-30 minutes or until golden brown, or use pastry to make small tarts.

Favourite Pepper Steak

1 lb. top ground beef
1-2 tbsp. vegetable oil
⅓ cup chopped green onions
1 clove garlic, minced
¼ cup cold water
3 med. green peppers, slivered
1 cup sliced Chinese cabbage
1½ cup beef stock
2 tbsp. cornstarch
2 tbsp. soya sauce

Cut beef in narrow strips. Heat oil in saucepan and brown meat slowly until well browned on all sides. Sprinkle with salt and pepper. Stir in green onions, garlic, green pepper and cabbage. Add beef stock and simmer covered, 10 minutes. Mix together cornstarch, soya sauce and water. Stir into meat mixture and cook 10 minutes longer, stirring until thickened.

Serve with medium or broad noodles. Simply cook noodles according to package directions. Drain and toss lightly with melted butter and snipped fresh parsley.

Delicious Hawaiian Meatball Casserole

1½ lbs. ground beef
2 eggs
¾ cup dry bread crumbs
2 onion Oxo cubes
½ cup boiling water
salt and pepper to taste

Combine beef, eggs, bread crumbs, onion cubes, which have been dissolved in the ½ cup boiling water, and seasonings. Shape into balls and brown in 2 tbsp. oil. Drain. Set aside.

1 14-oz. tin cubed pineapple
2 tbsp. corn starch
½ cup brown sugar
3 beef Oxo cubes
1½ cups boiling water
½ cup white vinegar
¼ cup ketchup

Drain pineapple, reserve juice. Combine corn starch, sugar and juice in a saucepan. Add beef cubes dissolved in boiling water, vinegar and ketchup. Cook stirring constantly until thickened and bubbly. Reduce heat. Stir in meatballs, cubed pineapple, and the following ingredients:

¾ cup small sweet gherkins
2 carrots, cooked & diagonally sliced
2 green peppers, cut in bite size pieces

Combine gently and heat thoroughly. Serve with rice. A very colorful dish.

Cabbage Rolls

Combine the following thoroughly:

2 lbs. ground lamb
1 lb. ground beef (or lean hamburger meat)
2 large onions - finely chopped
salt and pepper to taste
garlic powder or garlic clove (as desired)
1 cup uncooked rice

2-3 heads of cabbage, softened in boiling water (10-15 min.). Remove leaves and place 1-1½ tbsp. meat mixture in each and roll up loosely. Place cabbage rolls in roaster or heavy pot. Mix together 1 large can tomatoes (28 oz.) and 1 can tomato paste or ½-1 can (10 oz.) tomato soup. Pour this over cabbage rolls. Bake in slow oven 200°F, 2-3 hours, or on top of stove on low heat 2-3 hours.

Ham Lasagne

½ 16-oz. pkg. lasagne
¼ cup flour
¼ tsp. salt
¾ cup grated Swiss or Cheddar cheese
⅓ cup grated Swiss or Cheddar cheese
3 tbsp. butter or margarine
2 cups milk
⅛ tsp. pepper
1 egg, slightly beaten
2 cups cubed cooked ham
paprika

Cook lasagne according to package directions. Melt butter in a saucepan; add flour and seasonings and cook 1 minute, stirring constantly. Add milk; bring to boil, stirring constantly and cook 2 minutes longer.

Remove from heat. Add ¾ cup cheese and stir until sauce is smooth. Warm beaten egg with hot sauce and stir into sauce. Add the cubed ham. Pour part of the sauce into an 8" square pan.

Alternate the following layers three times: ⅓ lasagne and ⅓ sauce. Sprinkle with ⅓ cup cheese and parika.

Bake at 350°F about 20 minutes.

4 servings.

Broccoli Casserole

1 pkg. broccoli
2 med. onions
¼ cup butter
1 cup milk
2 tbsp. flour
½ tsp. salt
3 oz. cream cheese
½ cup shredded cheese
⅓ cup bread crumbs

Cook broccoli as directed on package. Cook onions which have been chopped in large pieces in boiling water for 5 minutes. Melt butter in pan, add milk, flour and salt. Beat till smooth. Add cheese. Stir till melted.

Place broccoli and onions in casserole dish. Mix in sauce. Top with shredded cheese, and bread crumbs. The bread crumbs can be moistened with a little butter.

Bake 45 minutes at 350 degrees.

Onion Soup Au Gratin

¼ cup butter
2 Spanish onions, thinly sliced
6 cups beef broth or consomme
salt and freshly ground pepper
2 cups grated Swiss cheese
2 tbsp. vegetable oil
1 tbsp. granulated sugar
¼ cup sherry
8 slices French bread toasted

In large saucepan, heat butter and oil over medium-high heat; add onions and sprinkle with sugar. Cook, stirring occasionally, for 15 to 20 minutes or until onions are soft and golden brown. Add broth and bring to boil; reduce heat and simmer, uncovered for 15 to 20 minutes. Add sherry. Taste and add salt and pepper, if necessary.

Ladle hot soup into 8 individual ovenproof bowls. Float bread slice in each bowl and sprinkle each with ¼ cup cheese. Broil 3 inches from heat until cheese is golden brown.

Makes 8 servings.

Newfoundland-Style Fried Rice

1 cup uncooked rice
4 tsp. salad oil
1 beef or chicken bouillon cube
1½ cups boiling water
½ tsp. salt (or to taste)
1 tbsp. soya sauce (or to taste)
1 med. onion (chopped)
½ green pepper (chopped)

Cook rice in oil until golden brown. Dissolve bouillon cube in boiling water; add salt and sauce. Add to rice, cover and cook for 20 minutes. Add remaining ingredients and ¼ cup more water, if needed. Cover. Cook 10 minutes longer.

Tasty Festive Steak Slices

2 lbs. round steak
garlic powder
meat tenderizer
onion powder
soya sauce
vinegar

Slice meat into thin strips. Sprinkle with spices and tenderizer. Place in a large bowl and marinate with ⅔ soya sauce and ⅓ vinegar (or to taste). Place in fridge for approx. 1 hour, turning now and then.

Fry quickly in oil at a high temperature. Drain meat and serve on a bed of rice.

Festive Tuna Salad

1 can condensed chicken broth
½ cup water
1 envelope unflavoured gelatin
2 large cans solid white tuna
6 hard cooked eggs (chopped)
1 jar diced pimento (drained)
3-4 large celery stalks (finely chopped)
1 medium avocado (sliced)
2 tsp. grated lemon peel
salt and pepper to taste
1 cup chilled whipping cream
lettuce

In a heavy large saucepan, mix chicken broth and water. Sprinkle gelatin on top and heat over low heat until dissolved, stirring constantly. Place in refrigerator until slightly thickened, about 50-60 minutes. Beat cream until stiff. Set aside.

Combine remaining ingredients and stir into gelatin mixture. Fold cream into tuna mixture. Pour into a 8x8 inch baking dish and refrigerate for 3-4 hours or until firm.

Cut into squares and place on lettuce leaves. You may also use a jelly mold.

Potato Salad

12 potatoes
1 med. onion
5 tbsp. salad dressing
2 tbsp. pickle relish
1 tin mixed vegetables

Cook potatoes; strain and mash. Then while potatoes are still hot, cream with salad dressing and finely chopped onion. Stir in pickle relish, if desired, and mixed vegetables. Place in salad dish. Garnish as you please. Cool in refrigerator.

You may omit tinned vegetables and add chopped hard boiled egg.

— TIP —

Don't throw out your pickle liquid. Mix it with oil for a delicious salad dressing.

Scalloped Potatoes

6 potatoes
2 tsp. salt
⅔ cup skim milk powder
2 tbsp. flour
⅛ tsp. pepper
2 cups water

Wash and peel two potatoes and cut them in thin slices. Place these potato slices in a greased baking dish.

Mix the flour, salt and pepper together. Sprinkle half the flour mixture over the sliced potatoes. Add 2 tbsp. margarine.

Wash, peel and slice two more potatoes into the baking dish. Sprinkle the rest of the flour mixture over the sliced potatoes.

Wash, peel and slice two more potatoes into the baking dish. Mix the skim milk powder and water to make skim milk. Pour the skim milk over the sliced potatoes.

Cover and bake in a moderate oven 350°F. After 45 minutes, take off the cover and continue baking untl potatoes are tender. 30 to 35 minutes.

6-8 servings.

Duchess Potatoes

Boil **1½ lb. potatoes.** Drain. Let dry. Add **¼ cup milk**. Beat with electric mixer until creamy. Add **2 egg yolks**, one at a time. Blend well. Add **½ cup fresh parmesan cheese, salt and pepper** to taste. Combine well. Place in a piping bag. Pipe onto a lightly oiled baking sheet. Brush tops with a slightly beaten **egg**.

Bake in a 400°F oven until golden brown.

Note: When piping, make to desired size and shapes. Eg: use rosette tip for an attractive presentation. Very nice!

Yule Time Chili Con Carne

Brown **1 lb. hamburger** with **1 tbsp. oil.** Add **1 large chopped onion** and continue cooking until onion is transparent. Drain off fat. Add the following ingredients:

1 tin tomato soup
1 tsp. salt
2 tsp. chili powder
1 tin kidney beans (14 oz.)
dash cayenne pepper
¼ tsp. oregano

Simmer — 30 minutes. Serve with hot rolls and salad.

Baked Mashed Potatoes

3 lbs. med. size potatoes, pared (about 9)
1½ tsp. salt
¼ cup packaged bread crumbs
1½ cups dairy sour cream
¼ cup butter or margarine
¼ tsp. pepper
1 tbsp. butter or margarine, melted

Cook potatoes in boiling water until tender. Drain thoroughly. Combine potatoes, sour cream, ¼ cup butter, salt and pepper in large bowl.

Beat at low speed with electric mixer until blended. Beat at high speed until light and fluffy. Pike lightly into a buttered 2-quart casserole. Cover and refrigerate overnight, if you wish.

Bake, covered, in a slow open (325°F) for 1 hour. Toss bread crumbs in 1 tbsp. melted butter. Sprinkle over potatoes. Continue baking, uncovered, 30 minutes.

Makes 8 cups.

Holiday Baked Beans

1 lb. white beans
¼ lb. salt pork
1 onion
1 tbsp. prepared mustard
4 tbsp. molasses
1 tsp. salt
pepper to taste

Pick over the beans; wash thoroughly.

Drain; cover with cold water; boil gently 1 hour; drain.

Place the onion and pork in the bean pot or in an oven dish. Pour in the beans.

Sprinkle with salt, pepper and mustard. Add the molasses and hot water to cover.

Bake, covered, for 6 hours at 300°F, adding water as necessary.

Remove the onion. (more molasses may be added in water if sweeter, darker beans are desired.)

Serve with your favourite bread.

— TIP —

Put a pinch of baking powder in your mashed potatoes and they will become nice and fluffy.

Breads & Puddings

Holiday Raisin Bread

2 pkg. yeast
1 cup lukewarm water
3 cups lukewarm water
1 cup molasses
¼ cup butter (melted)
12 cups or more of flour
2 tsp. sugar
¼ cup brown sugar
2 tbsp. salt
1 pkg. or more of raisins
spices if desired

Dissolve yeast in 1 cup of lukewarm water to which 2 tsp. of sugar has been added. Combine 3 cups lukewarm water, molasses and melted butter. Sift dry ingredients, add raisins and spices. Stir dissolved yeast into molasses mixture. Stir flour into mixture and knead for 10 to 12 minutes. Place in a greased bowl and let rise to about double in bulk for about 2½ hours. Divide dough to form into loaves. Place into greased pans and let rise for 1 hour. Bake at 400°F for about 30-35 minutes. Brush with melted butter while hot.

Christmas Bread

1 cup boiling water
½ cup butter
2 tsp. salt
½ cup sugar
1 tsp. sugar
½ cup lukewarm water
2 pkgs. dry yeast
2 eggs, lightly beaten
½ tsp. nutmeg
1 tsp. allspice
1 tsp. caraway seeds
6 cups flour
1 cup currants
¾ cup raisins
½ cup chopped citron

Combine boiling water, butter, salt and ½ cup sugar. Stir until sugar is dissolved and butter melted, and cool to lukewarm. Dissolve 1 tsp. sugar in ½ cup lukewarm water. Sprinkle in yeast and let stand 10 minutes. Stir well. Add to cooled mixture. Stir in eggs, spices and half of flour. Beat with a spoon until smooth. Add enough of remaining flour to make a soft but not sticky dough. Turn out on floured board and knead until smooth. Knead in fruit. Put in greased bowl, cover with a damp cloth and let rise in a warm place until double, 1 to 1½ hours. Punch down. Knead again a few times. Divide dough in two and shape into two round loaves. Put on greased cooking sheets. (Or shape into 2 regular loaves and put in greased 9x5x3 inch loaf pans.) Let rise in a warm place until double. Heat oven to 400°F and bake 10 minutes, then reduce temperature to 350°F and bake 50 minutes. Pour glaze (recipe follows) over loaves while still warm, and let it run down sides of loaves. Decorate with candied cherries and citron if desired.

Glaze

¾ cup sifted sugar
¼ tsp. almond or rum flavouring
2 tbsp. hot milk

Blend together and pour over warm bread, letting it run down sides.

— TIP —

Substitute for icing sugar: Combine 1 cup granulated sugar and one tablespoon cornstarch in a blender. Blend until powdery. Makes about 1½ cups.

Mini Fruit Loaves (or Christmas Wreath)

1 tsp. sugar
½ cup warm water
1 pkg. active dry yeast
1 cup skim milk
½ cup margarine
3 large eggs (beaten)
⅓ cup sugar
1¼ tsp. salt
1 tsp. cinnamon
4-5 cups flour
½ cup golden raisins
½ cup chopped cherries
½ cup mixed peel
½ cup chopped pecans

In a large bowl dissolve sugar in the warm water. Sprinkle yeast over top and let stand 10 minutes. Stir briskly with a fork. Heat milk and margarine. Stir to melt. Cook to lukewarm. Add to stirred yeast. Add beaten eggs, sugar and salt. Add cinnamon to about 2 cups flour, gradually stir into yeast mixture and mix until a soft, slightly sticky dough is acquired. Turn out onto a floured surface and knead for about 2-4 minutes, adding more flour as necessary. Place in a greased bowl and let rise in a warm place, until double in size - about 1½ hours. Punch down and knead in the fruit and nuts.

Place in greased mini loaf pans or regular size if you prefer. Bake at 375°F for 45-55 minutes, or until done. Remove from pans and let cool on racks. Then drizzle with icing sugar if you wish.

P.S. Instead of making loaves, shape dough into a Christmas wreath by cutting dough into 3 equal pieces. Shape into ropes and braid together and place on a greased cookie sheet. Shape into a ring pinching edges together. Let rise in a warm place for about 1½ hours. Brush with a mixture of 1 egg white, beaten slightly, with 1 tbsp. of water.

Bake at 375°F for 40-55 minutes or until done.

Drizzle with frosting when cool if desired.

— TIP —

Candles arranged in the centre of the table make an elegant, yet easy centrepiece. Place them atop a mirror for a stunning effect.

Raisin Orange Bread

Raisin Orange Bread should be described as a sweet dough product but since it has only ¼ cup (plus 1 tsp.) sugar in it, it is not all that sweet.

It might be compared to a raisin loaf for the uses to which you will put it.

When you serve this to your family or at a coffee party, your baking reputation will rise by leaps and bounds.

1 tsp. granulated sugar
½ cup lukewarm water
1 pkg. granular yeast (1 tbsp.)
½ cup milk
⅓ cup butter
¼ cup granulated sugar
1 tsp. salt
Rind and juice from 1 extra large orange (approx. 2 tbsp. rind and
1½ cups raisins (preferably bleached)
1 egg
3-3½ cups unsifted all-purpose flour (divided - see below)

In a one-cup measure dissolve the 1 teaspoon sugar in the lukewarm water. Sprinkle over yeast and let stand 10 minutes. Stir once.

Meanwhile heat and stir milk, butter, sugar and salt in a small pan until warm to the touch and butter melts and sugar and salt are dissolved. Pour into a large bowl. Stir in yeast liquid, orange rind and juice, raisins, egg and 2 cups of the flour. Blend then beat until smooth and elastic. Add 1 cup more flour and work into dough. Turn out on a lightly floured board and knead until smooth and elastic. If dough becomes sticky, sprinkle over some of the remaining half cup flour and knead in. (Approximaely 3¼ c. flour in all.)

Place dough in large greased bowl and rotate to grease all surfaces. Cover and let rise in warm place until doubled — about 1½ hours. Punch down dough and turn out on lightly floured board and knead again. Return to bowl, cover and let rest 10 minutes. Shape dough into a 19 inch roll which is just long enough to surround centre tube of a greased 12-cup bundt or tube pan. Press ends snugly together. (**Note:** you may use your tube pan with removable centre if necessary.) Let rise uncovered, until doubled — about 1 hour. Bake at 350°F 35 to 40 minutes or until when bread is tapped it sounds hollow. Remove from oven and immediately brush surface with melted butter. Let stand in pan no longer than 3 minutes then remove from pan and cool on cake rack.

Lovely to serve at a coffee or tea party.

— TIP —

When planning a cocktail party, allow about 5 or 6 hors d'oeuvres per person.

Easy Refrigerator Rolls

2 tsp. sugar
2 cups warm water
2 envelopes dry yeast
¼ cup soft shortening
½ cup sugar
2 tsp. salt
6-7 cups all purpose flour
1 egg

In large mixing bowl, dissolve 2 teaspoons sugar in warm water. Sprinkle on yeast and allow to stand 10 minutes. Add soft shortening, sugar, salt and half of the flour. Beat thoroughly for 2 minutes. Add egg and beat well. Mix in remaining flour with spoon or by hand until dough is easy to handle. Place in a greased bowl. Brush top with melted butter. Cover with waxed paper and clean towel. Place in refrigerator. Refrigerated, it will keep 5-6 days. When ready to make rolls, cut off required amount and place remainder in refrigerator. Shape dough into rolls while still cold. Brush with melted butter and let rise until doubled in bulk about 35 minutes. Bake 400°F 10-12 minutes.

Preparation time — 30 minutes **(4 doz. rolls).**

French Bread

6-7 cups flour
1 tbsp. salt
2½ cups water
2 tbsp. sugar
1 pkg. active dry yeast
1 egg white, beaten

Combine 2 cups flour, sugar, salt and yeast. Blend well. In small saucepan heat water until very warm. Add warm water to flour mixture. Blend at low speed until moistened. Beat 3 mins. at medium speed. Stir in enough flour to make a stiff dough on a lightly floured surface.

Knead in remaining flour until dough is smooth and elastic, about 10 mins. Place in greased bowl. Let rise until double in bulk, about 1 to 1½ hours.

Punch down several times to remove air bubbles. Let rest (covered) for 15 minutes. Divide into 4 equal pieces. Work dough to remove large air bubbles. Shape each piece into a 16" rope. Place in greased pans. With sharp knife make five ¼-inch deep slashes on each loaf. Brush with beaten egg white.

Cover and let rise in a warm place (e.g. oven) until tops of loaves are even with pan edges — approximately 40 to 50 minutes.

Preheat oven to 400°F. Bake for 15 minutes. Reduce oven temperature to 350° and bake 25 to 30 minutes more until loaves sound hollow when tapped.

Remove from pans immediately. Cool by laying loaves across pans.

Christmas Muffins

3 cups flour
½ cup sugar
2 tsp. baking powder
1 tsp. baking soda
dash salt
2 cups sour cream
⅓ cup skim milk
½ cup corn oil
½ tsp. almond extract
2 large eggs, beaten
1½ cups chopped frozen cranberries or partridgeberries
½ cup sliced blanched almonds
¼ cup golden raisins

In a large bowl, combine dry ingredients. In a separate bowl combine liquid ingredients. Fold into dry mixture just until moistened.

Fold in berries, one half of the nuts. Add raisins. Fill greased muffin tins ⅔ full. Place remaining nuts on top.

Bake in a 425°F oven, for approximately 40-45 minutes or until tester when inserted in centre comes out clean.

Cranberry Tea Buns

3 cups flour
5 tsp. baking powder
2 eggs
1 cup milk
¾ cup butter
1 cup cranberries or partridgeberries
½ cup sugar
1 tsp. vanilla
pinch salt

Take flour, butter, sugar, salt and rub together with baking powder. Then beat eggs, milk and vanilla. Add to flour mixture and mix. Sprinkle cranberries with flour and fold into batter. Cut out buns and bake at 400°F for 20-25 minutes.

— TIP —

To make sour milk or buttermilk, add 1 tablespoon of vinegar or lemon juice to one cup of milk.

Christmas Cranberry Nut Bread

¼ lb. butter
1 cup sugar
1 egg
1 cup warm milk
1 tbsp. vanilla
2 cups flour
½ tsp. salt
½ tsp. soda
1½ tsp. baking powder
1 cup coarsely chopped cranberries
½ cup chopped nuts

Cream butter and sugar, add egg. Mix well, then slowly add milk and vanilla.

Sift flour, salt, soda and baking powder together and add to first mixture. Then fold in chopped cranberries and nuts.

Bake in a greased and floured loaf pan for 1 hour at 350°F.

Lemon Raisin Tea Bread

½ cup margarine
1 cup sugar
2 large eggs
grated peel of 1 lemon
1½ cups flour
1 tsp. baking powder
½ cup milk
¼ cup chopped nuts
¼ cup golden raisins

Cream margarine and sugar thoroughly. Add eggs one at a time. Beat until light and fluffy. Add lemon peel. Sift dry ingredients together. Add to creamed mixture, alternately with milk. Fold in nuts and raisins. Pour into prepared loaf pan. Bake 350°F for 45-55 minutes or when tester inserted in centre comes out clean. Remove from oven and while still warm pierce holes in top and pour over the following glaze while still in pan:

¼ cup sugar
juice of one lemon and rind.

Combine well.

Cool for about 10 minutes before removing from loaf pan.

Christmas Orange Bread

½ cup butter or margarine
¾ cup granulated sugar
3 eggs
½ cup mashed bananas
½ cup orange juice
2½ cups flour (sifted)
4 tsp. baking powder
¾ tsp. salt
1½ cup mixed candied fruit
¼ cup raisins
¾ cup chopped nuts
confectioners' sugar
fruit to decorate

Cream butter or margarine, add sugar and blend. Add eggs, beat until light and fluffy. (Add one egg at a time, beating well after each addition.) Combine bananas and orange juice. Add to creamed mixture alternately with sifted dry ingredients mixed with fruits and nuts. Pack into greased and wax paper lined loaf pan 9x5x3 inches. Bake in moderate oven (350°F) 1 hour or until done. Cool about 20 minutes before turning out on rack. When cold, dust with confectioners' sugar mixed with a little milk. Decorate with citron and cherries.

Apricot Loaf

2 tbsp. butter or shortening
1 cup sugar
1 egg, beaten
3 cups flour
5 tsp. baking powder
½ tsp. salt
1 cup milk
1 cup dried apricots, soaked in water
½ cup nuts, chopped
Rind of 1 orange, grated (if desired)

Cream together butter or shortening with sugar. Add egg. Sift together flour, baking powder and salt. Add alternately with milk. Add 1 cup of dried apricots which have been soaked in water, drained and cut up fine and ½ cup of chopped nuts.

Put in loaf pan and let rest for 20 minutes. Bake at 350°F for 1 hour or until done.

Holiday Carrot Nut Bread

1½ cups sifted all purpose flour
¼ tsp. ground cinnamon
2 eggs beaten
1 tsp. vanilla
1½ cups grated carrots
1½ tsp. baking soda
¾ cup sugar
½ cup vegetable oil
½ tsp. salt
1½ cups ground pecans or walnuts

Sift together flour, baking soda and cinnamon. Add sugar, eggs, oil, vanilla and salt.

Blend in carrots and nuts with as few strokes as possible.

Turn into a greased 9x5x3 inch loaf pan. Bake in pre-heated 350°F oven for approximately 1 hour. Cool in pan for 10 minutes. Turn out on rack to cool completely.

Christmas Cherry Loaf

large pkg. cream cheese (8 oz.)
½ cups sugar
1 cup margarine
1 tsp. vanilla flavouring
1 tsp. almond flavouring
4 large eggs
2¼ cups cake & pastry flour
1½ tsp. baking powder
2 cups drained maraschino cherries (red & green, chopped)
½ cup ground almonds

In a large mixing bowl, blend cream cheese, sugar, margarine and flavourings. Add eggs one at a time, beating well after each addition. Gradually add two cups of flour and baking powder, mixing well. Toss the remaining ¼ cup flour with the cherries and nuts. Fold into batter.

Pour into two greased and lightly floured loaf pans. Bake in a pre-heated 325°F oven for 1-1½ hours or until tester inserted into centre comes out clean. Remove to wire rack and while still warm, drizzle with the following glaze: Mix ½ cup icing sugar with enough milk to make a thin glaze.

— TIP —

The secret to a high rising souffle is accomplished by the making of a collar. This is done by cutting a long strip of parchment paper, long enough to go completely around and overlap slightly. Fold the paper two to three times and place around dish. Tie in place. Fill mold up to the collar.

Tips for a Successful Christmas Pudding

TO STEAM

Spoon batter into a well greased mold (you may dust the mold with sugar if you wish). Fill ⅔ full and cover with greased tight-fitted lid, or waxed paper; over this place a dampened tea towel, which has been lightly sprinkled with flour. Tie towel in place, leaving room under cloth for expansion.

Set pudding on a rack or small flat plate or lid, in steamer or deep pot. Fill to about ⅔ full with boiling water, replacing water as needed. Cover and bring to a boil. Reduce heat and simmer gently for about 1-1½ hours or as directed, or until cake tester when inserted into centre comes out clean.

Remove waxed paper and towel. Unmold and garnish or glaze as desired. Serve warm or cold with your favourite sauce.

If not using immediately, store in a cool dry place, wrapped in plastic wrap and foil. Will keep for months if frozen. Thaw before reheating.

To-Reheat: Wrap in foil and place in a 350°F oven for approximately 1 hour, or until heated through, or re-heat in microwave by placing pudding on a serving plate. Cover with plastic wrap and heat on med. high for approx. 5 minutes or until hot. Let stand covered for about 3 minutes. OR: To re-heat place pudding back into a lightly greased mold. Cover as before and steam for about 30-60 minutes or until heated through!

TO FLAME PUDDING

Unmold warm pudding onto serving plate. Sprinkle lightly with sugar. Meanwhile warm ½ cup brandy in a small saucepan over low heat, just until it begins to vaporize or steam. DO NOT BOIL.

Pour the warm liquid over the pudding and light by carefully touching a long match to edge of the liquid on serving plate.

When finished flaming, decorate with a sprig of holly. Serve with your favourite sauce and enjoy.

SCREECH is a traditional Newfoundland alcoholic drink first brought to the island by Jamaican rum-runners centuries ago. You may substitute any dark rum in recipes calling for Screech.

Old Fashioned Christmas Pudding

1 cup flour
1 cup suet
½ cup molasses
1 cup currants
½ tsp. baking soda (dissolve in hot water and add last)
½ tsp. cloves
½ tsp. nutmeg
1 cup bread crumbs
½ cup brown sugar
1 cup raisins
1 cup mixed peel and cherries
1 egg (beaten)
1 tsp. allspice
1 tsp. cinnamon
½ cup milk

Mix all together in a deep bowl. Grease mold well and fill ¾ full. Cover and steam 2-3 hours in approximately 2 inches of water.

Serve with your favourite sauce.

P.S. If desired, add extra fruit, e.g. dates, figs, apricots, etc.

No Nonsense Christmas Puddin'

1 cup flour
1 cup bread crumbs
1 cup sugar
1 cup raisins
1 cup chopped apple
1 cup hot milk
1 cup butter
1 tsp. baking soda
1 tsp. each cloves, cinnamon and allspice

Mix all dry ingredients together except soda. Rub in butter. Add fruit. Add milk (to which soda has been added) and mix. Steam 3 hours covered with wax paper and then a wet cloth.

Spicy Raisin Pudding (Boiled)

1 cup minced suet
2 cups white flour
1 tsp. mace
3 tsp. cinnamon
1½ tsp. allspice
1 cup brown sugar
1 pkg. large raisins (11 oz.)
½ tsp. salt
3 oz. Screech
2 tbsp. molasses
3 tsp. baking powder

Combine all ingredients, adding a little water if necessary so batter won't be too stiff. Tie in a cloth and place in a pot of cold water. Add ¼ tsp. salt to water before putting pudding in. Let water come to a boil and steam pudding for about 2½ hours, covered. (Place pudding on a plate while in the pot.)

Vanilla Sauce

¼ cup butter or margarine
1 tbsp. flour
dash salt
1 tsp. vanilla
1 cup milk
½ cup white sugar
drop of rum may be added

Melt butter, add flour, dash of salt and vanilla. Add milk and sugar. Continue cooking over medium heat until thickened. Stir constantly.

Delicious served with your favourite Christmas pudding. You may sometimes double this recipe and freeze half for later.

Lemon Sauce

½ cup white sugar
1 cup boiling water
1 tbsp. flour
1 lemon, sliced thin

Combine sugar and flour. Slowly add 1 cup boiling water. Bring to a boil. Add lemon slices and continue to simmer a few minutes. Discard lemon slices, and serve sauce warm.

Caramel Sauce

4 tbsp. brown sugar
1 tbsp. butter
½ cup water
1 tbsp. flour
½ cup Screech

Blend sugar, flour and butter together. Stir in Screech and water. Boil, stirring constantly for a few minutes. Serve over pudding.

Rum Sauce

2 cups dark brown sugar
2 tbsp. butter
2 tbsp. Screech or add to taste
1 tsp. salt
2 cups water

Boil all together and thicken with a mixture of cornstarch and water.

Cakes & Cookies

Dark Christmas Cake

1 tbsp. allspice
1 tbsp. cinnamon
1 tsp. cloves
1 cup molasses
1 cup butter
1 cup sugar
5 eggs (well beaten)
3½ cups flour
½ tsp. salt
3 cups raisins
3 cups currants
1¼ cups dates
4 cups mixed peel
2 cups citron peel
1 tsp. baking soda
2 tbsp. hot water
¼ cup rum or brandy may be added

Steep spices in molasses over low heat. DO NOT BOIL, but the longer it is allowed to heat, the darker the cake will be. Let cool.

Cream butter and sugar well. Add the well beaten eggs, then the cooled molasses mixture. Add rum, if using.

Dust fruit well with ¼ cup of the flour called for in the recipe. Combine remaining flour and salt. Gradually add to the creamed mixture and blend well.

Stir in the floured fruit. Last of all mix the soda with the hot water, until dissolved. Add to batter.

Pour into a large baking pan lined with 3 layers of brown paper. An iron bake pot is best. It should be at least 10 inches wide and three inches deep. Bake at 275° oven for 3-3½ hours.

TIPS:

A pan of water placed in the oven when baking cakes helps keep them moist.

For fruit cakes — soak a cheese cloth in brandy, cherry, or fruit juice and place over cake. Wrap in foil and store. This brings out the old fashioned flavour.

Aunt Maud's Economical Boiled Christmas Cake

½ lb. butter
2 cups warm water
1 lb. mixed peel or fruit
1 tsp. cloves
1 tsp. cinnamon
2 cups brown sugar
2 lbs. raisins (or one lb. currants))
1 pkg. cherries
1 tsp. allspice
3 tbsp. cocoa

Place above ingredients in large heavy pot. Bring to a boil. Boil for 5 minutes. Simmer for approximately 15 minutes.

When cool add **3 cups flour, 1 tsp. baking powder, 1 tsp. baking soda.**

Bake 275° for 2½-3 hours.

P.S. I used large tube pan lined with greased brown paper. Truly moist and delicious. This cake will keep for months wrapped in foil in fridge.

Cherry Cake

1 cup butter
1½ cups sugar
4 eggs
1 tsp. vanilla
1 tsp. almond flavouring
1 tsp. lemon flavouring
3 cups flour
½ tsp. salt
1 tsp. baking powder
¾ cup warm milk
1½ cups floured cherries
(use some of the flour in recipe)

Cream butter and sugar well. Add eggs one at a time, beat until fluffy. Mix in flavourings. Combine dry ingredients together and add alternately with the warm milk. Fold in cherries.

Baked in a lined tube pan in a 325° oven for 1½ hours or until done (when cake tester inserted into centre comes out clean.)

— TIP —

Store dried herbs and spices in a cool, dark place or they will rapidly lose both flavor and color. The absolutely worst place to keep them is on a shelf over the kitchen stove where they get heated and cooled whenever you use the stove.

Fruity Pound Cake

1½ cups raisins
2 cups mixed candied fruits
⅓ cup whiskey
3½ cups sifted all-purpose flour
1½ tsp. baking powder
¾ tsp. ground nutmeg
1½ cups butter, softened
1¾ cups sugar
6 eggs
⅓ cup milk
1½ cups chopped pecans

Combine raisins, fruits and whiskey in a medium-size bowl. Let soak several hours.

Grease and flour a 10-inch tube pan. Set aside. Sift flour, baking powder and nutmeg. Lay aside.

Cream butter and sugar in a large bowl with electric mixer until smooth. Beat in eggs until light and fluffy (one at a time).

Stir in flour mixture alternately with milk, beating until smooth after each addition. Stir in fruits, whiskey and nuts. Turn into prepared pan.

Bake in preheated slow oven (300°F) for 2 hours and 10 minutes or until top springs back when lightly pressed with fingertip. Cool in pan on wire rack 20 minutes. Remove from pan; cool completely.

Wrap cake in whiskey soaked cheesecloth; overwrap in foil. Store in refrigerator 3 to 4 weeks, resoaking cloth as necessary. Decorate with chocolate curls and mandarin oranges if you wish.

Quick and Easy Fruitcake

9 cups corn flakes, crushed to make 3½ cups of crumbs
¾ cup chopped walnuts
⅓ cup chopped mixed peel
½ tsp. nutmeg
1 tsp. baking powder
1 can sweetened condensed milk
1½ cups mincemeat
1 cup raisins
1 cup dried currants
½ cup halved candied cherries
½ tsp. cinnamon
½ tsp. ground allspice
3 eggs

In large bowl, thoroughly combine all ingredients. Turn mixture into waxed paper-lined and greased 8x8x4 inch square baking pan. Spread batter evenly. Bake in 300°F oven for 1¾-2 hours or until toothpick inserted in centre comes out clean. Allow to cool 10 minutes in pan, then turn out onto wire rack to finish cooling.

Light Coconut Fruit Cake

2 cups coconut
1½ cups diced candied pineapple
1½ cups slivered almonds
1 tsp. baking powder
1 cup butter
1 tsp. almond extract
1 cup pineapple juice
1½ cups halved candied cherrries
1½ cups light raisins
2⅔ cups all-purpose flour
1 tsp. salt
2 cups granulated sugar
4 eggs

Grease and line 9 or 10 inch tube pan with brown paper. Grease paper. Set aside.

Combine coconut, fruits, nuts and 1 cup flour. Mix well until fruit is separated and coated with flour. Set aside.

Combine remaining flour with baking powder and salt.

Cream butter, sugar and almond extract thoroughly. Add eggs, one at a time, beating well after each addition.

Add dry ingredients to creamed mixture alternately with pineapple juice, making 3 dry and 2 liquid additions; combine lightly after each. Add floured fruit mixture. Mix well.

Spread batter evenly into prepared pan. Bake in 275°F oven for 2½ to 3 hours or until toothpick inserted in centre comes out clean. Keep a pan of hot water on bottom of oven while baking to prevent cake from drying out.

Cook cake in pan. Remove from pan, peel off brown paper and store, well wrapped in foil, in cool dry place.

Note: Cakes can also be baked in two 9x5 inch loaf pans.

Ruby's Strawberry Tea Bread

(Makes two breads.)

1 cup margarine
1½ cups sugar
1 tsp. vanilla
4 eggs
3 cups flour
1 tsp. salt
1 tsp. cream of tartar
½ tsp. baking soda
1 cup strawberry jam
½ cup sour cream
2 tsp. grated lemon rind
1 cup chopped walnuts

Cream butter, sugar and vanilla until light and fluffy. Add eggs one at a time, beating well after each addition. Sift flour, salt, cream of tartar and soda. Add to creamed mixture alternately with jam, sour cream and lemon rind, beating well after each addition.

Stir in ¼ cup chopped walnuts.

Divide batter into two greased and floured 9x5" loaf pans.

Sprinkle tops with remaining nuts. Bake 350°F, 60-70 minutes or until top springs back when lightly touched in center. Cool 10 minutes. Remove from pan.

Festive Dark Fruit Cake

1 cup finely ground salt pork
1 cup hot strong coffee
1 cup sugar
1 tsp. cinnamon
1 tsp. nutmeg
1 tsp. allspice
1 tsp. baking soda
2 eggs (beaten)
⅔ cup molasses
3 cups of flour
5 cups of fruit (includes 2 cups yellow raisins, 2 cups whole cherries, 1 cup dates)

Place the ground pork in a bowl and pour the hot coffee over it. Let it stand until cold. Then stir in spices, sugar and soda, well beaten eggs and molasses. Add all but 2 tablespoons of the flour to the mixture and mix until well blended. Toss the fruit with the reserves 2 tablespoons of flour until it is all coated then add the floured fruit to the batter mixture. Mix well and bake in a well greased and floured pan.

This recipe makes a large cake and an Angel Food pan is just the right size. Bake 2 hours and 15 minutes in a slow oven (300-325°).

Holiday Dark Fruit Cake

1 pkg. raisins
1 tsp. cinnamon
1 tsp. cocoa
½ tsp. cloves
1 tsp. vanilla
1 pkg. mixed peel
1 tsp. allspice
1 cup brown sugar
½ cup butter

Add 1 teaspoon of soda to 1 cup of hot water, and place in a saucepan with the above ingredients and let boil. After boiling, let cool and mix with:

1 cup chopped nuts
2 cups dates
2 tsp. baking powder
1½ cups cherries
1½ cups flour

Bake 1¾ hours at 350°F in a 10-inch tube pan.

— TIP —

Did you know that vinegar softens cuticals and conditions nails? Simply dip your fingernails into a solution of one half cup of water and two teaspoons white vinegar. Pat dry and apply nail polish.

Glazed Fruit Cake

1 cup chopped candied fruit
1½ cups red & green cherries
1 cup chopped dates
1 lb. raisins
1½ cups chopped walnuts
¼ cup flour (for dusting)
4 cups flour
½ tsp. baking soda
½ tsp. nutmeg
½ tsp. cloves
½ tsp. cinnamon
½ tsp. allspice
½ cup margarine
1 cup sugar
1 cup dk. corn syrup
3 large eggs
½ cup brandy
½ tsp. vanilla
½ tsp. almond flavouring
½ cup light corn syrup for glaze

Combine fruit and nuts. Coat well with ¼ cup of flour. Set aside. In a large bowl combine 4 eggs, flour, baking soda and spices; lay aside. Cream margarine, sugar and dark syrup. Add eggs one at a time, beating well after each addition. Stir in brandy and flavourings. Gradually add the flour mixture, blending well. Fold in floured fruit and nuts. Combine well.

Pour batter into a greased and lined tube pan (brown paper makes the best liner). Cover tightly with foil. Bake in a 300°F oven for about three hours or until cake tester when inserted in center comes out clean.

Remove to wire rack and let cool completely. Then turn out and remove the paper. Wrap in plastic wrap then in foil and store in a tightly covered container. Store for at least one month for best results.

If you intend to glaze — do so about a day or two ahead.

Bring light syrup to a slow boil. Brush over top and sides of cake. Garnish with candied cherrries or other fruit.

Tangy Lemon Raisin Loaf

½ cup sugar
¼ cup margarine or butter
2 large eggs
1¼ cups all purpose flour
1 tsp. baking powder
½ tsp. salt
½ cup milk
½ cup raisins
2 tsp. grated lemon rind
⅓ cup honey
¼ cup lemon juice

Cream margarine and sugar well or until fluffy. Add eggs one at a time and beat until thoroughly blended. Sift flour with baking powder and salt. Add this mixture to the creamed mixture alternately with the milk, beginning and ending with the dry ingredients. Fold in the raisins and grated lemon rind.

Pour into a greased 9x5x3" loaf pan. Let stand for 15 minutes before placing in oven.

Bake 350°F for approx. 50 minutes or until loaf is browned and done.

Dissolve the honey in the lemon juice and spoon over the hot loaf.

Cool in the pan on a rack for 20-30 minutes before turning out.

Delicious Christmas Fruit Bars

½ cup chopped cherries
1 cup currants
½ cup mixed fruit
½ cup chopped nuts
¼ cup orange juice
1½ cups flour
½ tsp. salt
1 tsp. baking powder
½ tsp. cinnamon
¼ tsp. nutmeg
½ cup butter
1 cup brown sugar
2 beaten eggs
1 tsp. vanilla

In a medium bowl, combine fruit and nuts. Pour the orange juice over all. Set aside.

Sift the dry ingredients. Lay aside. Cream butter and sugar. Add eggs and vanilla, and beat until light and fluffy. Add flour mixture and mix well. Stir in the fruit-nut mixture. Spread into a greased 9-inch pan and bake 375°F (350°F if using glass dish) for 25 minutes. When cool, cover with a thin layer of butter icing (to follow). Cut into bars and garnish with red and green cherries.

Basic Butter Icing

1 cup icing sugar
2 tbsp. butter
2 tbsp. milk
1 tsp. vanilla
1 egg yolk (optional) (makes for a richer icing)

Cream 2 tbsp. of the icing sugar with the butter. Add milk and vanilla. Gradually add remaining icing sugar and mix until smooth, adding more milk or icing sugar until desired consistency is obtained.

Santa Claus Cookies

4 cups sifted all-purpose flour
½ tsp. baking soda
¼ tsp. salt
1 cup butter or margarine
2 cups sugar
3 eggs
1 tsp. vanilla
red and white tinted icing sugar
red cinnamon candies
shredded coconut
green sugar (use food colouring)

Sift together flour, baking soda and salt. Cream butter; slowly add and beat in sugar and continue beating until well blended. Add eggs, one at a time, beating well after each addition; blend in vanilla. Add sifted dry ingredients gradually; blend well. Cover bowl; chill dough in the refrigerator several hours or until firm enough to roll.

Set oven for moderate, 350°F. Grease cookie sheets. On a lightly floured board, roll out chilled dough, ¼ inch thick. Cut with floured Santa Claus cookie cutter; place on cookie sheets. Bake 8 to 10 minutes, or until cookies are golden. Run spatula under cookies to remove from sheets. Cool on wire racks. Decorate with icing, candies, coconut and sugar.

Makes about 4 dozen.

Frosty Christmas Tree Cookies

3¾ cups sifted all-purpose flour
½ tsp. salt
2 tsp. ground ginger
2 tsp. ground cloves
1 cup sugar
½ cup molasses
colored decorating sugar
1 tsp. baking soda
2 tbsp. cocoa
3 tsp. ground cinnamon
1 cup butter, softened
1 egg
sugar icing (recipe follows)

Sift flour, baking soda, salt, cocoa, ginger, cinnamon and cloves. Lay aside.

Beat butter, sugar, egg and molasses in a large bowl with electric mixer until fluffy-light. Stir in flour mixture until well-blended. Wrap dough in plastic wrap or foil; refrigerate several hours or overnight.

Preheat oven to 350°F. Roll out dough, ⅓ at a time, on a lightly floured surface to a ¼-inch thickness. Cut out with floured large Christmas tree cutter. Brush off excess flour; place cookies on lightly greased cookie sheets. Repeat with remaining dough. Gather up scraps for second rolling.

Bake in a preheated moderate oven (350°) for 8 minutes or until edges are browned. Let cookies cool a few minutes on cookie sheets. Remove to wire racks with a spatula; cool completely. Dip small clean brush into Sugar Icing and "paint" cookies. Sprinkle with colored sugars.

Makes 3 dozen cookies.

Sugar Icing

Combine 1 pkg. (1 lb.) confectioners' sugar, 1 tsp. vanilla and ⅓ **cup water** in a medium-size bowl; stir until smooth. Add more water, a teaspoon at a time, until icing is spoonable and flows easily.

Makes about 2 cups.

Christmas Cherry Shortbread

1 cup butter
2 cups flour
¾ cup brown sugar
yolk of 1 egg

Cream butter and sugar. Fold in egg yolk and add flour. Stir and knead mixture until soft and pliable. Cut with cookie cutter into desired shapes.

Garnish with red and green cherries.

Bake 375°F until golden brown.

Mom's Favourite Shortbread

½ cup icing sugar
½ cup corn starch
1 cup sifted flour
¾ cup butter or margarine

Sift dry ingredients together in large bowl.

Blend in butter with spoon. Mix until soft. Pat out on lightly floured board and cut into desired shapes with cookie cutters. Place on ungreased cookie sheet.

Bake in 300°F oven for 20-25 minutes or until edges turn lightly brown.

Note: Shortbread is very light in color. Pale. Never brown.

Snowballs

Put in double boiler **1/4 cup milk, 8 marshmallows.** Cook until marshmallows are dissolved, stirring constantly. Remove from heat but keep mixture standing in hot water. Dip **12 halved marshmallows,** one at a time in mixture. Roll in **1½ cups shredded coconut.** Put on waxed paper.

Nanaimo Bars

BASE:

2 squares semi-sweet chocolate
2 cups graham wafer crumbs
½ cup melted margarine
1 egg (beaten)
1 tsp. vanilla or almond flavouring
2 tbsp. sugar
½ cup chopped nuts
1 cup coconut

Melt and cool chocolate. Combine remaining ingredients. Add chocolate and mix well. Press into a 9-inch baking dish. Chill while preparing the following filling. (This makes for a thick base — therefore you may wish to adjust the desired thickness by decreasing the amount of ingredients placed in the baking dish. Save remainder for another 8 or 9 inch base.)

FILLING:

¼ cup margarine
2 tbsp. custard powder
2 cups icing sugar
3 tbsp. milk

In a deep mixing bowl, cream margarine. Add custard powder and icing sugar alternately with the milk. Mix to desired consistency, or until smooth. Spread gently over base. Chill for 15-20 minutes. Then spread with the following:

4 squares of semi-sweet chocolate
1 tbsp. margarine

Melt, then pour over filling. Place in refrigerator until set, then cut into bars. These freeze well.

— TIP —

Substitute for unsweetened chocolate: 1 oz., 3 tablespoons unsweetened cocoa plus 1 tablespoon butter, margarine or shortening. For semisweet chocolate: Same as above and add 3 teaspoons sugar.

Holly Wreaths

¼ cup butter or margarine
¼ tsp. green food colouring
4 cups corn flakes cereal
½ cup light corn syrup
¼ cup granulated sugar
tiny red cinnamon candies

Line baking sheets with waxed paper before you start.

In medium saucepan, mix butter, corn syrup, food coloring and sugar.

Cook over medium heat, stirring constantly, until sugar dissolves and mixture boils. Boil for 4 minutes, stirring often. Remove from heat and add corn flakes. Fold together until well coated.

Using greased spoon, drop by rounded tablespoons onto waxed paper lined cookie sheets. Shape into wreaths about 2 inches in diameter. Rinse hands with cold water if mixture is hot to handle. Decorate with red candies for berries while wreaths are still sticky.

Makes about 18 wreaths.

Easy Chewy Cherry Squares

1 envelope (½ pkg.) pie crust mix
1 cup flaked coconut
¾ cup chopped nuts
½ cup wheat germ
¼ cup all-purpose flour
¼ cup lightly packed brown sugar
2 tbsp. margarine, melted
1 (19 oz.) can cherry pie filling
1 can sweetened condensed milk

Prepare pie crust mix according to package directions (or use your own favourite recipe), making until combined but still crumbly. Pat on bottom of ungreased 13x9-inch baking pan.

Bake at 400°F for 8-10 minutes or until lightly browned.

Combine coconut, nuts, wheat germ, flour, sugar and margarine in small bowl. Set aside.

Spread pie filling evenly over crust; pour sweetened condensed milk evenly over pie filling.

Sprinkle coconut mixture on top.

Bake at 350°F for 35-40 minutes or until lightly browned.

Cool before cutting.

Makes one 13x9-inch pan.

Giant Crisp Chocolate Chip Cookies

The Children will LOVE them!

2 cups flour
1 tsp. each baking soda and salt
1 cup butter or margarine, softened
1½ cups sugar
1 egg
1 tsp. vanilla
1 pkg. (12 oz.) semi-sweet chocolate pieces (2 cups)
1 cup chopped nuts

Mix flour, baking soda and salt; set aside. In large bowl cream butter until fluffy. Gradually beat in sugar until light. Beat in egg and vanilla until blended and fluffy. Stir in flour mixture, chocolate and nuts until well mixed. Shape in 2-inch balls; place 3 inches apart on ungreased cookie sheets (6 on each sheet).

Bake on middle rack in preheated 350°F oven 20-23 minutes or until golden and edges are lightly browned. Cool completely on cookie sheet. Store covered in dry cool place.

Makes 21 4-inch cookies. Watch them disappear!

Christmas Oatmeal Fruit Drops

1½ cups all-purpose flour
1 tsp. salt
¾ tsp. baking soda
1 tsp. cinnamon
¾ cup margarine, softened
1 cup sugar
2 eggs
⅓ cup milk
1½ cups quick or instant oats
1 cup raisins
1 cup chopped candied cherries
½ cup chopped nuts, optional

Combine flour, salt, soda and cinnamon; stir to blend well.
Cream margarine, sugar and eggs thoroughly.
Add flour mixture to creamed mixture alternately with milk.
Stir in oats, raisins, cherries and nuts.
Drop mixture by teaspoonfuls onto lightly greased baking sheets.
Bake at 375°F for 12-14 minutes.
Makes about 4 dozen.

Desserts

Yule Baked Alaska (with a Nfld. Flavour)

2 qts. chocolate ice cream or desired flavour
1 tsp. cream of tartar
2 tbsp. Screech
5 large bananas
8 egg whites
1 cup sugar

Pack ice cream into a narrow 6-cup mold. Cover and freeze until form. Unmold ice cream onto a cold board (do not use metal). Peel 3 bananas. Cut in half lengthwise and again into halves crosswise. Press into sides of molded ice cream. Peel remaining bananas. Cut into slices and pile on top of molded ice cream. Place in freezer, while preparing meringue.

In a large mixing bowl, beat egg whites with cream of tartar, until soft peaks form. Gradually beat in sugar and continue beating until very stiff, approximately 15 minutes. Remove ice cream from freezer. Spread meringue all over bananas and ice cream, making sure meringue touches board all around. Make a depression 1 inch deep in top of meringue.

Bake in pre-heated oven 450°F for 3 minutes, or until meringue is lightly golden. Warm Screech and pour into depression in top of meringue. Ignite and serve.

P.S. Impressive dessert served at your New Year's Eve Party.

Black Forest Log

¼ cup cocoa
1 cup cake flour
3 lg. eggs
1 cup granulated sugar
⅓ cup water
1 tsp. vanilla
2 cups whipped cream
½ cup confectioner's sugar
1 tbsp. Kirsch
1 14-oz. tin pitted red cherries
1 tbsp. strong coffee
2 tsp. cocoa
glace cherries and grated chocolate for decoration

Grease 10x15 inch jelly roll pan. Line with wax paper. Butter the paper and sprinkle with flour. Mix cocoa and flour together. Set aside.

Beat eggs at high speed, until thick and lemony (3-5 mins.) Beat in granulated sugar, gradually. Lower speed and add water and vanilla. Gradually add flour and cocoa, beating until smooth. Pour into pan, spreading evenly into corners. Bake on middle rack, 375°F (approx. 12-15 mins.) or until toothpick inserted in cake comes out clean. Loosen sides of cake and turn out onto a tea towel. Remove wax paper and quickly but gently (while still hot) roll up cake and towel together from narrow end. Cool, seam side down, on wire rack. When cake is almost cool, unroll carefully and sprinkle with 4 tsp. of syrup (recipe follows). Leave cake for approximately 20 minutes.

Meanwhile, whip 1 cup cream and ¼ cup confectioner's sugar until cream stands in peaks. Set aside 2 tbsp. cream for decoration and fold 1 tbsp. Kirsch into rest. Spread cream over cake. Sprinkle with well-drained chopped cherries and roll up cake. Place cake gently on serving plate by using the towel on which it rests (seam side down).

Whip together 1 cup cream, coffee, cocoa and ¼ cup confectioner's sugar, until cream stands in peaks.

Cover cake with cream, giving the appearance of the rough surface of a log. Place three cherries on cake, and add a few drops of **green** food coloring to the rest of the cream and make 2 holly leaves on each side of cherries. Sprinkle cake with grated chocolate.

Put in fridge until ready to serve.

SYRUP (for above)

3 tbsp. granulated sugar
2 tbsp. Kirsch
¼ cup cherry juice (reserved in can)

Boil juice and sugar until dissolved. Cool and stir in Kirsch.

Pineapple Loaf

Slice a **jelly roll** very thin and line sides and bottom of a large size loaf pan with slices.

Drain juice from 19 oz. can crushed pineapple and add **3 envelopes of gelatin** — lay aside.

Separate **3 eggs.** Beat the yolks with ½ **cup sugar** in saucepan. Add **1½ cups milk** and place over heat. Add **gelatin** and bring to a boil. Remove from heat, add **juice of 1 lemon** and **1 tsp. vanilla** and cool.

Beat whites of eggs and fold in, also folding in pineapple.

Pour mixture over jelly roll slices. Let set in refrigerator. When ready to serve, unmold on plate and cover with whipped cream and dream whip.

Slice and serve.

Christmas Baked Apples

4-6 large baking apples
1 cup prepared mincemeat
1 cup brown sugar (firmly packed)
1 cup water
2 tbsp. margarine
½ tsp. nutmeg
½ tsp. cinnamon

Core apples but do not pierce completely through. Cut strip from top of each. Place in a 13x8" greased baking dish. Fill cavity of apples with the mincemeat. In a medium saucepan place remaining ingredients. Bring to a slow boil.

Pour over apples in dish. Bake uncovered in a 350°F oven for approx. 1 hour. Baste occasionally. Serve with a dollop of fresh cream, if desired.

Candy Cane Parfait

3 med. candy canes
1 cup icing sugar
4 cups whipping cream
chocolate sauce

Crush 1 candy cane and place in top of double boiler along with 1 cup whipping cream; heat over hot water, stirring until melted.

Whip remaining 3 cups cream, adding sugar gradually, until thick. Slowly pour melted candy cane mixture into whipping cream, beating gently. Taste and adjust sweetening.

Pour into 9x5 inch loaf pan or ice cube trays and freeze. When parfait is partially frozen, crush remaining candy canes and stir in. Freeze until firm. To serve, scoop into individual serving dishes and spoon chocolate sauce over.

Makes 6 servings.

Apple Coffee Cake

2¼ cups flour
¾ cup sugar
¾ cup margarine
½ tsp. baking powder
½ tsp. baking soda
1 tsp. cinnamon
1 large egg (beaten)
¾ cup sour milk
1 tin apple pie filling (19 oz.)

In a large bowl, combine flour and sugar. Cut in margarine until crumbly. Remove about ½ cup. Set aside. To remainder of dry ingredients add baking powder, baking soda and cinnamon.

Combine egg and sour milk, add to dry ingredients. Mix until moistened. Spread ⅔ of batter over bottom and partly up side of a greased 9" springform pan. Pour pie filling gently over this. Spoon remaining batter over apple filling. Sprinkle reserved crumb mixture over this. Sprinkle lightly with nutmeg.

Bake in a 350°F oven for 50-60 minutes or when toothpick inserted in center comes out clean.

Let cool in pans before removing sides.

Apple Pie Delight

4-5 large tart apples
2 tbsp. flour
½ cup sugar
½ tsp. cinnamon
dash nutmeg
1-9" frozen pie shell
½ cup brown sugar
½ cup flour
¼ tsp. cinnamon
½ cup margarine

Peel, core and thickly slice the apples. Combine next four ingredients and toss with the apples. Place in pie shell. Combine brown sugar, flour and spice. Cut in margarine until crumbly. Sprinkle over apples.

Place on a cookie sheet on bottom shelf of oven. Bake in a pre-heated 400°F oven for about 10 minutes. Reduce heat to 350°F and bake for another 40 minutes or until apples are tender.

Serve hot or cold with a dollop of fresh cream or sour cream if desired.

— TIP —

A dash or two of vanilla on a cotton ball gives a refreshing fragrance to your refrigerator.

Beverages

Holiday Eggnog

6 eggs, separated
1 pt. brandy or whiskey
⅓ cup dark rum
nutmeg
1 pt. chilled milk
¾ cup sugar
1 pt. chilled heavy cream, whipped

Beat egg yolks until thick. Slowly add and beat in brandy and rum. Stir in milk. Whip egg whites until very foamy. Gradually add and beat in sugar; beat just until egg whites form soft, shiny peaks. Fold egg whites into brandy mixture; fold in cream. Chill in the refrigerator.

At serving time, pour the mixture into a chilled bowl and sprinkle with nutmeg. **Makes about 24 servings.**

Golden Eggnog

6 eggs, separated
¾ cup sugar
1 qt. chilled milk
nutmeg
1 tbsp. vanilla
1 pt. chilled heavy cream, whipped

Whip egg whites until very foamy. Gradually add and beat in sugar. Beat just until egg whites form soft, shiny peaks. Beat egg yolks until thick. Fold in egg whites. Slowly stir in milk and vanilla. Fold cream into egg mixture. Chill in the refrigerator.

At serving time, pour mixture into a chilled bowl; sprinkle with nutmeg.

Makes about 24 servings.

Chocolate Rum Eggnog

1 qt. rich chocolate ice cream
4 oz. dark rum

Warm ice cream in heavy saucepan over moderate heat till just below the boiling point. Stir in dark rum until well mixed. Serve in eggnog cups.

Quick & Easy Rum Eggnog (for 12)

Pour in large punch bowl, **1 qt. fresh or canned eggnog.** Pour in **12 oz. amber rum.** Fold in **1 cup (8 oz.) whipped heavy cream.** Chill in refrigerator. Stir.

Top individual servings with **nutmeg.**

— TIP —

When serving punch, use a block of ice in preference to cubes — they melt too rapidly and tend to dilute the flavour of the punch.

Spiced Cranberry Punch

Here's a special Christmassy punch to make your party festive.

½ cup granulated sugar
3 cinnamon sticks
4 whole allspice berries or allspice seasoning
1 cup orange juice
2 cups rum
1 cup water
6 whole cloves
2½ cups cranberry juice cocktail
½ cup lemon juice
3 cups ginger ale

In small saucepan, mix sugar, water, cinnamon, cloves and allspice; bring to boil, reduce heat and simmer for 5 minutes. Strain and chill.

At serving time, combine spiced syrup and fruit juices in punch bowl; stir to blend. Add ginger ale and rum.

Makes 10 servings.

Majestic Punch

Prepare the syrup for this punch a day ahead so flavors have a chance to mingle.

½ cup granulated sugar
1 cinnamon stick
peel of 1 lemon and 1 orange
1 cup orange sections
4 cups dry white wine, chilled
4 cups sparkling wine, chilled
½ cup corn syrup
3 cups water
1 can (19 oz.) pineapple tidbits
1 cup lemon juice
1 cup Kirsch

In 2-quart saucepan, blend sugar, corn syrup, cinnamon, water and lemon and orange peels. Over medium heat, bring syrup to boil; boil for 2 minutes. Cover and refrigerate overnight to develop flavors.

At serving time, strain syrup mixture into large chilled punch bowl. Add undrained pineapple tidbits, orange sections, lemon juice, kirsch and wines.

Makes 16 cups.

Brandied Cider

2 qts. apple cider
¾ tsp. whole allspice
1¼ cups brandy
Orange or lemon slices (optional)
1½ tsp. whole cloves
2 three-inch pieces stick cinnamon

Combine cider, cloves, allspice and cinnamon in a large saucepan. Bring slowly to boiling; lower heat. Simmer 15 minutes. Remove spices. Add brandy.

Pour into punch bowl or individual cups. Add orange or lemon slices to each cup of cider, if you wish.

Makes 8 servings.

Granny's Tia Maria

2 cups boiling water
2½ cups white sugar

Boil above for 1 minute. Add **5 tbsp. camp. coffee** and **1 tsp. vanilla.** Chill. Ten add **26 oz. alcohol.** Pour into liqueur bottle.

Irish Cream Liqueur

¼ tsp. vanilla
1½ tbsp. cocoa or chocolate syrup
¼ tsp. coconut extract (optional)
3 eggs

Put in blender. Mix together **1 cup (8 oz.) rye whiskey, 1 tin sweet condensed milk** and **1 cup whipping cream.** Blend until smooth and keep refrigerated.

Shape before pouring. Will keep approximately 4-5 days.

Christmas Candy

Candy Making Tips

Fudges are made up of tiny crystals, the finer the crystals, the smoother the fudge. Avoid excess stirring while cooking, and do not beat or agitate the cooling syrup after cooking until it has reached the correct temperature for beating. The use of brown sugar, syrup, cream of tartar or vinegar in a candy mixture tends to retard crystallization of the syurp; butter and cream also have this effect. Always choose fudge recipes which contain at least one of these ingredients.

It is wise to use a candy thermometer for accurate results. Test the thermometer before you use it. Stand it in boiling water for a few minutes, should read 212°F. If not and the thermometer registers more, add the difference to the temperature specified in the recipe. If registers less, deduct the difference. During cooking, the bulb of the thermometer should be completely immersed in the mixture and should not rest on the bottom of the pan.

If you do not have a candy thermometer, use the cold-water test: Remove mixture from heat and drop about ½ tsp. of it into a bowl filled with cold water (not ice water). Let it stand for a minute, then check for firmness by rubbing mixture between fingers. Check the guide below:

SOFT BALL: 235°F-240°F - Syrup forms a soft ball (in water); will gradually disappear when rubbed between fingers.

HARD BALL: 250°F-265°F - Syrup forms a hard ball (in water), which holds its shape when rubbed between fingers.

FIRM BALL: 244°F-250°F - Syrup forms a firm ball (in water). May flatten when rubbed, but not disappear.

HARD CRACK: 290°F-310°F - Syrup becomes very brittle, both in and out of water.

SOFT CRACK: 270°F-290°F - Mixture separates into threads, that are hard but not brittle when placed in cold water.

THREAD: 230°F-234°F - Syrup spins a 2-inch thread as it falls from the spoon.

Caramel Cream Divinity

A smooth, rich candy which keeps better than Divinity. Bring to a boil in a large heavy pan **2 cups cream.** Remove from heat and stir in **3 cups sugar** and **1 cup white corn syrup.**

Return to heat and cook slowly. When the candy boils, cover and cook for about 3 minutes until the steam washes down any crystals which may have formed on the sides of the pan. Uncover and cook slowly, without stirring, to the soft-ball stage, 238°F. Remove syrup from heat. Cool to 110°F. Beat until very stiff. Beat in **1 cup pecans.** Pour the candy into a buttered pan. Cut when cool.

Yield: Approximately 2 pounds.

Divinity

3 cups granulated sugar
⅔ cup corn syrup
¾ cup boiling water
2 egg whites
½ tsp. vanilla
½ cup chopped nuts
¼ cup chopped maraschino cherries, drained dry

Put sugar, syrup and water into a saucepan. Heat slowly, stir until sugar is dissolved. Boil to firm ball stage — 250°F; cool slightly.

Beat whites stiff, gradually add the syrup. Place on heat over hot water and continue beating until mixture begins to thicken.

Add vanilla, nuts and cherries; pour into buttered pan.

Note: Mixture may be dropped from a teaspoon on buttered pan; place bowl over hot water to keep mixture soft.

— TIP —

When you are making candy or preparing sugar syrup, keep a tall glass of hot water next to the stove. Dunk the candy thermometer into the water after you test the syrup. This will prevent the sugar from hardening and clinging to the thermometer.

Coconut Fudge

3 cups brown sugar
¼ cup butter
¾ cup evaporated milk

Combine these ingredients and boil until mixture reaches the soft ball stage. Remove from stove; add **2 cups coconut** and **2 tsp. vanilla.** Beat for one minute. Pour into a greased nine inch square pan. Cut when cool.

Vanilla Fudge

2 cups sugar
⅔ cup heavy cream
1 cup milk
4 tbsp. corn syrup
¼ tsp. salt
1 tsp. vanilla

Cook sugar, cream, milk, syrup and salt in a saucepan slowly to boiling.

Continue cooking on low heat until the mixture reaches a temperature of 234°F or the soft ball stage.

Cool without beating to a temperature of 110°F or until mixture feels just warm.

Add vanilla; beat until mixture loses its gloss and thickens; pour into a greased pan. Chopped cherries may be added.

Note: Instead of using heavy cream and milk, the following may be substituted:

(a) **1½ cups milk** plus ½ **cup butter.**

(b) **1¼ cups 18% cream,** plus **milk to make a total of 1⅔ cups.**

— TIP —

When you are making candy, you can prevent the mixture from boiling over by buttering the upper third of the saucepan.

Jiffy Fudge

1⅔ cups granulated sugar
2 tbsp. butter or margarine
½ tsp. salt
¾ cup evaporated milk
1½ cups chocolate chips
¼ lb. finely cut or miniature marshmallows
1¼ tsp. vanilla
¾ cup chopped nuts

Chop nuts, butter a 9x9x2-inch pan. Combine sugar, butter, salt and milk in 2 qt. saucepan. Bring to boil on medium heat, then cook 5 minutes, stirring all the time.

Remove from heat, add chocolate chips, marshmallows and vanilla. Beat at once, using mixer on No. 5 speed about 11/2 minutes only until mixture will hold shape. Blend in nuts. Turn into pan. Cool and cut in squares.

Makes about 4 doz. pieces

Old-Fashioned Fudge

2 cups granulated sugar
1 cup milk
½ tsp. salt
2 sqs. unsweetened chocolate
2 tbsp. light corn syrup
2 tbsp. butter or margarine
1 tsp. vanilla
1 cup chopped nuts

Chop nuts, butter a 9x9x2-inch pan. Combine sugar, milk, salt, chocolate, corn syrup in heavy saucepan. Cook and stir over low heat until sugar dissolves. Then cook slowly, stirring frequently to soft ball stage (238°F). Remove from heat.

Add butter, cool without stirring to 1100F or to lukewarm. Add vanilla. Place in large bowl of mixer. Beat on No. 11 speed until no longer shiny and mixture will hold shape. Beat in nuts. Turn at once into pan. Cool, cut in squares.1 cup of miniature marshmallows may be added before turning into pan.

Makes about 4 doz. pieces

— TIP —

Unwrapped hard candies will not stick together if you sprinkle then with a little granulated sugar before packing them into a container. Always select a container with a tightly fitting lid to exclude the air.

Chocolate Fudge Deluxe

3 cups sugar
1 envelope gelatin
1 cup milk
½ cup light corn syrup
3 sqs. unsweetened chocolate
1¼ tbsp. butter or margarine
2 tsp. vanilla extract
1 cup coarsely chopped walnuts

Butter an 8x8x2 inch pan. In a 3½ sq. saucepan, mix sugar with dry gelatine. Add milk, corn syrup, chocolate and butter. Cook over medium heat, stirring frequently to 238°F on candy thermometer or until a little in cold water forms a soft ball. Remove from heat, pour into a large mixing bowl, stir in vanilla. Cool 25 minutes. Beat with wooden spoon until candy thickens, stir in walnuts. Spread in prepared pan. Let cool and cut into squares.

Five Minute Fudge

Combine ⅔ **cup undiluted evaporated milk** with **1⅔ cups sugar** in saucepan; heat to boiling. Cook 5 minutes, stirring constantly. Remove from heat.

Add **2 cups miniature marshmallows, ½ cup walnuts, 1½ cups semi-sweet chocolate chips** and **1 tsp. vanilla.** Stir until marshmallows melt. Pour into buttered pan. Cool and cut into squares.

10 Minute Fudge

3 sqs. (1 oz. each) unsweetened chocolate
4 tbsp. margarine or butter
½ cup corn syrup
1 tbsp. water
1 tsp. vanilla
4½ cups icing sugar - sifted
⅓ cup skim milk powder
½ cup chopped nuts

Melt chocolate and margarine or butter in a 2 qt. double boiler over medium heat.

Add corn syrup, water and vanilla to the melted chocolate mixture.

Sift the icing sugar and skim milk powder together and add to the mixture. Stir over medium heat until the mixture becomes very smooth. Remove from heat and add nuts. Pour into lightly buttered 8x8 inch pan. Chill. Cut in squares.

Peanut Butter Fudge

2 cups sugar
½ cup milk
2 tbsp. water
⅓ cup peanut butter
1 tsp. vanilla
1 tbsp. butter

Cook sugar, milk, water slowly, stir occasionally to 236°F or until a few drops form a soft ball when dropped in cold water. Remove from heat, cool till hand can be held at bottom of pan.

Add peanut butter, vanilla and butter. Beat until smooth. Put in greased pan. Cut in squares when cool.

Grandma's Favourite Fudge

2 cups dark brown sugar
1 tsp. vanilla
1 cup coconut
½ cup milk
⅔ cup butter or margarine
approx. 3 cups rolled oats

Boil together the brown sugar and milk for approximately 5 minutes while stirring constantly.

Remove from stove and add vanilla, butter or margarine, coconut and rolled oats. Mix well, spread in 8 inch dish. Place in fridge until firm. Cut in squares.

Keep fudge in fridge until ready to serve.

French Fudge

3 cups semi-sweet chocolate chips
1½ tsp. vanilla extract
1 can sweetened condensed milk
dash salt
½ cup chopped nuts, optional

In top of double boiler, melt chocolate over boiling water, stirring occasionally. Remove from heat; stir in sweetened condensed milk, salt, vanilla and nuts.

Spread mixture evenly into waxed-paper lined 8x8 inch baking pan. Chill 2 hours or until firm. Turn fudge onto cutting board, peel off paper and cut into squares. Tightly cover any leftovers.

Makes about 1¾ pounds.

Mom's Fabulous Nut Fudge

2 cups sugar
¼ cup butter or margarine
16 lg. marshmallows
¾ cup evaporated milk
¼ tsp. salt
1 6-oz. pkg. (1 cup) chocolate chips
1 tsp. vanilla
1 cup chopped nuts

Mix sugar, butter, marshmallows, evaporated milk and salt in a heavy 2-quart saucepan. Cook, stirring constantly, over medium heat to a boil (mixture will be bubbling all over top). Boil and stir 5 minutes more. Take off heat.

Stir in chocolate chips until completely melted. Stir in vanilla and nuts. Spread in buttered 8 inch square pan. Cool. Cut into pieces.

Brown Sugar Fudge

2 cups light brown sugar
1 tbsp. cornstarch
few grains salt
1 tbsp. butter
⅓ cup sweet cream or evaporated milk
1 tsp. vanilla

Combine all ingredients except the vanilla. Boil to the soft ball stage. Take from the heat; add vanilla and beat until creamy. Pour into a buttered 8 inch square pan. Mark into squares when still warm.

Note: ½ cup coconut, chopped nuts, raisins or cherries may be added.

Microwave Cashew Delight

1 cup granulated sugar
½ cup corn syrup
1 cup cashew nuts (halved)
1 tsp. margarine
1 tsp. almond flavouring
1 tsp. baking soda

Place sugar and corn syrup in a 1½-2 quart micro-safe measuring jug. Microwave on High for 4-5 minutes, or until sugar dissolves and mixture bubbles. Carefully stir in nuts and cook for 3-5 minutes longer or until mixture is a golden brown. Stir in margarine and flavouring. Add baking soda and stir until foamy. Pour at once onto a prepared lightly greased foiled-lined cookie sheet. Spread with a greased spatula. When completely cooled, peel off foil and break into pieces. Store in fridge in an airtight container.

Aunt Clare's Homemade Christmas Chocolates

¼ lb. margarine
1 tin cream
1 pkg. chocolate chips (6 oz. semi-sweet)
2 cups icing sugar
3 cups (approx.) coconut (fine)
¼ block parowax (melted over double boiler)

Cream butter and sugar well. Add cream and coconut and form into balls. Place in fridge until firm.

Melt chocolate chips and parowax in top of double boiler. Dip balls in chocolate mixture, gently with tongs. Place on wax paper and place in fridge. When ready to serve place individual chocolates on tiny decorative paper cups.

P.S. You may roll mixture around a cherry before dipping in chocolate.

Maple Cream

2 cups sugar
2 cups brown sugar
1 tbsp. flour
½ tsp. salt
1 cup rich milk
2 tbsp. butter
1 cup chopped nuts
½ tsp. vanilla

Mix first 4 ingredients in a large saucepan, add milk and butter, and bring to the boiling point.

Continue cooking mixture until it reaches the soft ball stage or a temperature of 236°F; grease an 8-inch square pan.

Cool without stirring to a temperature of 110°F or until mixture feels just warm.

Beat until mixture loses its gloss; add vanilla and nuts; pour quickly into pan.

— TIP —

When chopping nuts in a blender or food processor, add a tablespoon of flour for each cup of nuts to keep them from forming clumps.

Toasting nuts have a better flavor when baked into cakes. Spread the ground nuts on a flat pan and put them in a preheated 350°F oven for eight to ten minutes until they are lightly browned. Stir with a fork to distribute the heat evenly.

Apricot Coconut Candy

¾ cup dried apricots
¾ cup flaked coconut
½ tsp. grated lemon rind
½ tsp. grated lemon rind
1 tbsp. orange juice
⅜ cup granulated sugar or
¾ cup finely chopped nuts

Wash apricots, cover with boiling water. Let stand 5 minutes. Drain well. Grind apricots and coconut in food chopper using medium blender. Add orange rind, lemon rind and orange juice to ground fruit. Knead. Mix until well blended.

If candy seems dry, add enough additional juice to moisten. If it's too moist, work in small amount of icing sugar, 1 teaspoon at a time. Shape candy in 1 inch balls. Roll in granulated sugar or chopped nuts.

Makes 2 dozen.

Peanut Brittle

2 cups sugar
½ cup light corn syrup
1 cup water
2 cups peanuts
1 tsp. butter or margarine
1 tsp. vanilla
¼ tsp. baking soda

In a large heavy saucepan over low heat, combine first three ingredients. Cook until sugar is dissolved. Continue cooking without stirring until soft ball stage is reached.

Add peanuts and cook to the hard crack stage. Then add butter, vanilla, and soda. Stir just until combined. Pour at once using a buttered spatula onto a greased cookie cheet, spreading to edges of pan. Let cool then break into pieces.

Almond Bark (Microwave Way)

1 cup blanched nuts
1 tsp. butter
1 lb. white chocolate
1 tsp. almond flavouring

Place nuts and butter in a micro-safe measuing jug. Cook on High for 3-5 minutes, stirring twice. Separately cook chocolate on High for 2-4 minutes or until softened. Stir in flavouring. Add nuts and pour onto wax paper-lined cookie sheet.Refrigerate until set, then break into pieces.

Popcorn Balls

Offer small guests a popcorn ball as they leave the dinner table.

6 cups popped popcorn
¾ cup water
½ tsp. vinegar
1 cup granulated sugar
¼ cup light corn syrup
green or red food coloring (optional)

Place popcorn in large bowl.

In medium saucepan, mix sugar, water, corn syrup and vinegar; bring to boil. Cook, covered, for about 3 minutes until steam washes down sides of pan.

Uncover and cook, without stirring, to hard-crack stage (290°F/140°F on candy thermometer). Remove from heat and add red or green coloring, if desired. Pour immediately over popcorn. Stir gently with wooden spoon to coat popcorn.

Buffer your hands and press candied popcorn into small balls (try not to press so hard that you mash the popcorn). Let balls cool on waxed paper.

Wrap each in clear or colored cellophane or plastic wrap. Tie with colored string.

Makes about 12 popcorn balls.

Molasses Bull's Eyes

3 tbsp. butter
2 cups molasses
⅔ cup white sugar
1 tbsp. vinegar
pinch baking soda

Place in saucepan, stir until sugar is dissolved. Boil until mixture is brittle when tried in cold water. Turn out in a shallow pan, and when cool enough to handle pull until light coloured. Cut in small pieces using scissors.

— TIP —

To preserve the flavor of ground coffee, store it in your freezer.

Store popcorn in freezer. Pops better and no wasted kernels.

Hors d'oeuvres

Canapes

A canape consists of three sections: A base, a covering and some decoration. For the base you can use store-bought crackers and thins, or you can make your own from day-old bread, sliced thinly and cut into whatever shape and size you want (cookie cutters are useful here).

Toast or fry in butter, on one side only and spread lightly with butter. For coverings, you can use pate, shrimp, smoked salmon, slices of cheese, or anything else that takes your fancy.

For decoration, use chopped egg (yolk and white chopped separately), strips of red or green pepper, narrow pipings of mayonnaise, capers, finely chopped herbs such as parsley or chives, thin strips of cheese.

Festive Party Loaf

1 loaf unsliced white bread (preferably a day old) 24 oz. loaf
2 tomatoes thinly sliced
cream cheese, approx. ½ lb.
stuffed olives, sliced and sprigs of parsley for decoration
ham and celery filling
curried egg filling
avocado filling
light cream

Trim all crusts from the loaf. Cut bread lengthwise into four thick slices. Spread each slice with butter. Spread bottom slice with ham and celery filling. Top with second bread slice. Spread with egg filling. Top with slices of tomato and third bread slice. Spread with avocado filling. Top with remaining bread slice.

Mix cream cheese. Add enough cream so cheese will spread easily. Beat until smooth.

Spread on top and sides of loaf.

Garnish with olive slices and parsley or desired garnish.

Keep in fridge until ready to serve.

Cut in slices.

FILLINGS:

Ham and Celery Filling: Combine 1 cup cooked ham, ½ cup finely chopped celery and enough mayonnaise to moisten.

Curried Egg Filling: Combine 4 finely chopped hard-cooked eggs, ½ tsp. curry powder and enough mayonnaise to moisten.

Avocado Filling: Mash 2 fully ripe avocados; add 2 tbsp. French dressing. Stir until well blended.

You may substitute any of the above fillings for any of your favourites, e.g. tuna, chicken, turkey, etc.

Finger Lickin' Mini Pizzas

4 English muffins, toasted
dried oregano
1 cup diced cooked ham
1 8-oz. tin tomato sauce
½ green pepper
1 cup shredded Mozzarella cheese

Spread each muffin half with the sauce. Sprinkle with oregano. Place some ham and green pepper (rings or cut up, whichever is desired) on top. Sprinkle with cheese.

Place on baking sheet. Broil 4 inches from heat until cheese melts, approximately 4 minutes.

May be cut into bite size pieces or served as is!

Frosty Pine Cone Spread

FILLING:
1 can (5 oz.) crab meat, drained and flaked
4 hard-cooked eggs, finely chopped
2 tsp. lemon juice
1 tsp. finely chopped onion
1 can (4 oz.) shrimp, drained and chopped
½ cup mayonnaise
2 tbsp. finely chopped sweet red pepper
freshly ground black pepper and cayenne pepper

FROSTING:
½ cup softened cream cheese
¼ cup mayonnaise

GARNISH:
1 cup whole almonds
2 sweet red pepper rings

FILLING: In large bowl, mix together seafood, eggs, mayonnaise, red pepper, lemon juice, onion, and black pepper and cayenne to taste. Cover and chill for several hours. Remove from refrigerator and shape into large "pine cone" on serving platter.

FROSTING: Combine cream cheese and mayonnaise until well blended. Spread thin layer over entire surface of pine cone.

GARNISH: Insert pointed ends of almonds into frosting in uneven rows to resemble the "leaves" of a pine cone. Cover and chill until serving time. Garnish rounded edge of cone with pepper rings.

Serve with crackers.

Makes 2½ cups

Pickled Eggs

3 cups white vinegar
1½ tsp. salt
1 tsp. black peppercorns
12 hard-cooked eggs
1½ cups water
1 tsp. mustard seed
2 tbsp. sliced ginger root or ½ tsp. celery seed

Combine all ingredients except eggs in a saucepan and simmer, uncovered, for 10 minutes. Strain and cool. Pack eggs in sealable containers and pour liquid over eggs to cover.

Let stand at least 2 days before using. Pickled eggs may be kept for several weeks at room temperature, but cool storage is recommended.

Festive Stuffed Eggs

Peel **hard-boiled eggs,** slice lengthwise, scoop out the yolks and slice a very thin sliver from bottom of white halves so they will rest evenly on the tray.

For a red filling, mash up the **egg yolk** with enough **mayonnaise** to obtain the right consistency and add some **paprika** and **tomato paste** for color. Pipe into egg halves and decorate with tiny leaves cut from **green pepper.**

For the green filling, pipe **pureed asparagus tips,** seasoned to taste, into he egg halves and top with strips of **pimento.**

Holiday Cheese Ball

1 8-oz. pkg. cream cheese, softened
½ cup finely chopped walnuts
1 tsp. grated onion
⅛ tsp. ground red pepper
¾ cup shredded Cheddar cheese
½ cup shredded Gruyere cheese
1 tsp. Worcestershire sauce
½ cup chopped parsley

Beat cream cheese until fluffy. Stir in Cheddar and Gruyere cheese, walnuts and onion, Worcestershire, and red pepper. Shape mixture into ball. Wrap in wax paper and chill 2 hours or until firm.

Then unwrap and roll in parsley until evenly coated. Wrap and refrigerate.

Before serving let stand at room temperature for approximately 30 minutes.

Serve with your favourite crackers or on french bread.

— TIP —

For large scale entertaining, such as a big dinner party, making a time schedule can ease your mind and help you remember everything.

Yule Puffs

(With a cheese flavour)

½ cup butter
1 cup water
½ tsp. salt
1 cup sifted all-purpose flour
3 large eggs
2 tbsp. finely grated Swiss cheese

Add butter to the salted water and bring to a boil. When the butter has melted, add the flour all at once, stirring briskly until the mixture forms a thick ball around the spoon and is free from the side of the pan. Remove from heat and cool slightly.

Beat in the eggs one at a time until the dough is smooth and glossy. Stir in the grated cheese.

With a pastry bag and ½ inch tube, pipe dough onto an ungreased baking sheet in small mounds about ¼ to 1 inch in diameter. Bake in preheated 400°F oven until mounds are nicely puffed and browned (about 20 minutes). Pierce sides of puffs with the tines of a fork and leave them in the oven with heat off and door ajar for 10 minutes to dry. Cool on a wire rack.

Makes about 3 doz. puffs.

Fill with any of the following: tuna, crab or chicken, mixed with diced celery and salad dressing.

Pigs in Blankets

Cocktail Sausages
Pastry (below)

1 cup flour
½ tsp. salt
2 tsp. baking power
2½ tbsp. shortening
½ cup milk, or enough to make soft dough

Mix dry ingredients; cut in shortening and add milk. Knead dough a couple of times. Roll or pat out to desired thickness (roll thin).

Cut into about 2 inch squares and spread with mustard.

Place a sausage in centre and roll diagonally and seal. Place on cookie sheet in 400°F oven until golden brown, approx. 8-10 minutes.

Chicken Liver Pate

(makes about 3 cups)

½ cup margarine
1 lb. chicken livers
1½ cups mushrooms (coarsely chopped)
¼ cup chopped parsley
¼ cup chopped green onions
½ tsp. dry thyme leaves
dash salt
½ cup dry red wine
1 cup soft margarine

Melt ½ cup margarine in a large frying pan. Add chicken livers, mushrooms, parsley, green onions, thyme and salt. Cook over medium heat, stirring frequently until livers are cooked but still pink in centre. Add wine. Bring to a boil. Cover and simmer for 5 minutes. Cool. Place some of the mixture into blender. Cover and blend until smooth, stopping and scraping down sides when needed with a rubber spatula. Cream the remaining margarine and add to the chicken liver puree. For best results, chill for several hours or overnight. Remove from fridge about 30 minutes before serving.

Pate can be frozen for later use if desired.

Beef Tongue

3 or 4 lbs. fresh beef tongue
1 tbsp. vinegar
6 whole cloves
6 peppercorns

Wash tongue, place it in a deep kettle and cover with boiling water. Add vinegar, cloves and peppercorns. Simmer until fork easily penetrates the center of the tongue (from three to four hours). Let cool in the water in which it was cooked. Then remove and peel off the skin.

Serve cold or with sauce.

Note: A smoked tongue may be prepared in the same way, but soak it overnight before cooking.

Serve with crackers and cheese.

Seafood Cucumber Snacks

1 large seedless cucumber
1 tin crab meat or lobster
2 tbsp. salad dressing
salt and pepper to taste

Slice cucumber into ¼ inch slices. Mix seafood with the dressing and seasonings. Place about 1 tsp. of mixture on each slice of cucumber.

Cover and refrigerate for up to 6 hours.

Delicious!

Festive Sweet 'n Sour Meatballs

1 lb. lean ground beef
1 egg, slightly beaten
1 tsp. salt
dash pepper
2 tbsp. oil
1 med. onion, sliced
1 med. green pepper, cut in strips
1½ cups pineapple juice
⅓ cup reg. barbecue sauce
1½ tbsp. cornstarch
2 tbsp. water

Lightly combine first 4 ingredients; form into 16 meatballs.

Brown meatballs in oil; remove from pan. Saute onion and green pepper until tender-crisp.

Return meatballs to pan. Stir in pineapple juice and sauce.

Cover; simmer 15-20 minutes, or until meatballs are cooked.

Combine cornstarch and water; add to sauce; stir and cook over medium heat until clear and slightly thickened.

Makes 4 servings.

Marilyn's Sausage Ball

2 - 6" Polish sausages (grated)
1 large pkg. cream cheese
1 small pkg. cream cheese (for topping)
1 tbsp. Worchestershire sauce
1 tbsp. mustard
1 tbsp. salad dressing
2 tbsp. chopped onion, finely grated
2 tbsp. dill pickle, finely grated
2 tbsp. dill pickle juice

Mix all but small pkg. of cream cheese. Roll into two 6" balls. Freeze until ready to use.

Add **2 tbsp. milk** to the cream cheese. Spread over balls. Roll in crushed nuts.

Place on serving plate surrounded by a variety of cocktail crackers.

Crap Dip

2 pks. cream cheese (8 oz. each)
1 can crab meat (7-oz.) drained
⅓ cup ketchup
½ cup salad dressing
1 tbsp. Worchestershire sauce
½ tsp. garlic powder
¼ tsp. pepper

Place all ingredients in a blender. Mix until smooth. Makes about 3 cups.

Serve on crackers for an enjoyable snack.

Sweet and Sour Chicken

Boil **1 lb. chicken breasts** for 15-20 minutes. Cut in chunks.

Batter:

2 eggs
1 tbsp. baking powder
¾ cup cold water
1 cup flour
1 tsp. salt

Beat eggs lightly. Sift flour, baking powder and salt together. Add water. Mix until combined. Add meat. Deep fry 5-10 minutes or until golden brown.

Sauce:

⅔ cup water
⅓ cup vinegar
2 tbsp cornstarch
1 cup brown sugar
3 tbsp. ketchup
¼ cup cold water

In a saucepan combine water, brown sugar, vinegar and ketchup. Heat to boiling. Thicken with cornstarch dissolved in cold water. Add dash of ginger. Serve over chicken balls.

Balls may be precooked and dropped into hot fat for one minute to reheat.

Honey-Garlic Chicken Wings

2 lbs. chicken wings
⅓ cup soya sauce
½ cup chicken broth
2 tbsp. minced garlic or 1 clove garlic
½ cup honey
⅛ tsp. ginger
1 tsp. ketchup

Broil chicken wings until brown and place in a large saucepan. Combine remainder of ingredients, blend well and pour over chicken wings. Simmer for 1 hour or until sauce thickens. Turn chicken wings after ½ hour.

Delicious served with fried rice or as a nibbler.

Crab and Bacon Rolls

1 can (5 oz.) crab meat, drained and flaked
1 tbsp. minced onion
1 tsp. lemon juice
¼ tsp. salt
½ cup fine breadcrumbs
2 tbsp. tomato juice
1 tsp. dried parsley flakes
1 egg beaten
12 slices bacon, cut in half

In medium bowl, combine all ingredients except bacon. Mix thoroughly. Form into balls, about 1 tsp. each. Wrap bacon slice around each, securing with toothpicks.

Broil 4 inches from heat, turning frequently, until bacon is crisp.

Makes 24 hors d'oeuvres.

Holiday Vegetable Dip

1 tub sour cream
½ tsp. garlic powder
1 tsp. grated onion
1 tsp. grated celery
½ cup mayonnaise
1 pkg. (1 envelope) onion soup (sifted)
1 tsp. grated carrot

Place in large bowl and mix together lightly. Keep refrigerated until ready to use.

Arrange your favourite cut-up raw vegetables (e.g. carrot sticks, celery, cauliflower, broccoli, radish roses) around a bowl of dip. Very attractive — tasty and nutritious.

Holiday Nippy Bacon Dip

1 pkg. cream cheese, softened
⅓ cup. reg. barbecue sauce
6 slices bacon, cooked and crumbled
½ cup mayonnaise or salad dressing
1 tbsp. minced onion

Blend cheese and mayonnaise until smooth; stir in sauce, bacon and onion. Cover, chill.

Serve as a dip with raw vegetables, crackers or potato chips.

Makes about 2 cups.

Olive-Filled Cheese Balls

The zing of pimento-stuffed green olives inside a coating of cheese makes these appetizers conversation pieces. They are good when made with ripe olives, too.

1 cup (4 oz.) shredded sharp Cheddar cheese
½ cup all-purpose flour, unsifted
25 med. size pitted ripe or stuffed green olives, well drained
2 tbsp. butter or margarine, softened
dash of cayenne

Beat together cheese and butter until well blended and creamy.

Stir in flour and cayenne. Wrap a teaspoonful of dough around each olive, covering completely. Place 1 inch apart on ungreased baking sheet; bake, uncovered, in a 400°F oven for 15 minutes.

Makes about 25 appetizers.

Honey Garlic Ribs

4 lbs. side spare ribs (cut into 2" pieces)
½ cup soya sauce
½ tsp. garlic powder
1 jar garlic sauce (13 oz.)
¼ cup honey
2 tbsp. corn starch

Place ribs, soya sauce, garlic powder in a large saucepan. Half cover with water. Cover and bring to a boil. Reduce heat and simmer for about 15-20 minutes or until ribs are tender. Drain off part of the water.

Combine corn starch with enough water to make a smooth paste. Add to the jar of garlic sauce. Add honey. Mix well. Gradually pour into the rib mixture. Combine well. Continue cooking, stirring periodically until sauce is thick.

— TIP —

If your honey crystallizes, put the uncovered jar in a saucepan of hot water and heat over a low flame until it i smooth again.

INDEX

Main Dishes

Breads & Puddings

Cakes & Cookies

- Notes -

- Notes -

- Notes -

EXTRA COPIES OF

Newfoundland Christmas Cook Book

may be ordered from:

HILLCREST PUBLISHING
P.O. Box 77
North River, NL
A0A 3C0

for $10.50 each

Other cookbooks: - 64 Pages

- Newfoundland Homestyle & Traditional Recipes
- Newfoundland Homestyle Muffins & Quickbreads
- Newfoundland Favourite Blueberry Recipes
- Newfoundland Cookie Lovers Cookbook
- Newfoundland Desserts Galore
- Newfoundland Microwave Cooking

All are available for $10.50 each from the above address (includes postage, handling and tax). Sorry, no C.O.D. orders from the above address.